Teaching Parkour Sports in School Gymnastics

Sascha Rochhausen

Teaching Parkour Sports in School Gymnastics

A Practical Handbook of Parkour & Freerunning Instruction for Indoor Gymnastics Classes with Children and Teenagers

Bibliographic information from the German National Library: the German National Library has recorded this publication in the German National Bibliography; relevant bibliographic details can be obtained from its website: http://dnb.ddb.de

1st edition 2011
Author: Sascha Rochhausen
Translated into English by: Richard Brightbart
Concept and typesetting: Sascha Rochhausen
Cover design, layout and illustrations: Sascha Rochhausen
Photographs: Sascha Rochhausen, Lennart Paape (p. 63 centre),
Copyright © 2009 by Sascha Rochhausen, Oevenum;
All rights reserved. Duplication in whole or in part requires the explicit permission of the author.

Printed in Germany
Produced and published by: Books on Demand GmbH, Norderstedt

Sales:
E-Mail: info@parkoursport.com
www.parkoursport.com

ISBN 978-3-8423-7564-2

Acknowledgements

I would like to express my gratitude to the many people who helped me in writing this book, whether by testing out the exercises, imparting constructive criticism, correcting the text, suggesting improvements, or providing me with photographic images. The following people, in particular, deserve special mention:

Lars Christiansen
David Dwyer
Malte Hansen
Dirk Harder
Jan Hille
Henning von Holdt
Lennart Paape
Julian Paulsen
Wehna Roeloffs
Michel Schade
Ihno Schroth
Parkour sports basic course 2008/2009

I would also like to express my special thanks to Rolf Lindemann and to my family.

Please note

The author shall not be liable in any way whatsoever for any accidents, injuries or damage of any kind occurring in connection with information contained in this book.

Unless otherwise indicated, the use of the grammatical masculine form always additionally implies the feminine.

Additional Materials may be downloaded from www.parkoursport.com (-> Materials).

Author

Sascha Rochhausen
Born: 1974
Teacher of physical education

rochhausen@parkoursport.com

Contents

1. Introduction 9
    1. Origins of parkour 10
    2. The names of the moves 11
    3. Parkour is varied.. 11
    4. A successful trend.. 12
    5. Parkour sports in school gymnastics 12

2. Basic Moves 15
    1. Notes on basic moves 16
    2. Descriptions of moves and variations 18

3. Discussion 23
    1. Philosophy.. 24
    2. The term 'parkour sports'... 25
    3. The transfer problem.. 25
    4   The case for parkour sports.. 28

4. Teaching Methodology 29
    1. Teaching time 30
    2. Location... 30
    3. Safety.. 30
    4. Move exercises 31
    5. Differentiation 31
    6. Promoting independence... 31
    7. Parkour exercises in large groups 32
    8. Example of organising equipment.. 33

5. Sequence of Activities in a Typical Sample Lesson 35
    1. Warm up.. 36
    2. Main training.. 37
    3. Concluding game 38
    4. Agility training and relaxation.. 38

6. Illustrations and Symbols 39
    1. List of gymnastics apparatus 40
    2. Symbols and abbreviations 41

7.	Sample Lessons	43
	1. Balancing and Precision Jumps	44
	2. Simple Jumps	49
	3. Reverse Vaults	55
	4. Dash Vault and Underbar	60
	5. Spiral Underbar	65
	6. The Roll	69
	7. Wall Run	76
	8. Cat Leap and Wall Up	79
	9. Combining Movements	83
	10. Wall Spin	87
	11. Wall Flip	92
	12. Wall Up and Turn Vault	97
	13. Climbing, Muscling Up and Jumping	101
	14. Wall Spin Backwards and Obstacle Roll	106
	15 Timed Parkour Exercises	110
	16. Parkour Sports and Performance	113
	17. Theory Unit: Parkour and Freerunning	116
8.	Parkour Games	123
9.	Relaxation exercises	131
	1. Torso – front	132
	2. Torso – back	133
	3. Torso – hips and buttocks	134
	4. Torso – side	136
	5. Legs	137
	6. Arms	138
	7. Shoulders and neck	139
10.	Bibliography and References	141
	1. Internet addresses	142
	2. Films	142
	3. Bibliography	143
11.	Index	145

Foreword

"I never thought I would enjoy doing gymnastics", was how one enthusiastic pupil summed up the parkour sports moves he had just learned in that day's PE lesson. He is unlikely to have responded the same way if the teacher had announced, "Today we are going to practice the tucked jump!" Indeed, the simple fact that parkour sports are now being taught successfully in schools can be seen as proof that young people are still capable of finding enjoyment in classic gymnastics moves. By combining parkour and gymnastics, sports teachers have at last begun finding an exciting way of re-integrating long-forgotten exercises, such as the dash vault or speed vault, into their teaching programmes. All but ignored in recent years, these moves possess great exercise value, and are ideal as transitions to more well-known exercises.

Parkour sports combines all three of parkour's common current forms: classic parkour, freerunning, and competitive 'parcouring'. But more than that, by combining parkour elements with more traditional exercises, a non-standardised, non-competitive aspect can be incorporated into gymnastics. As a trend sport, parkour is gradually gaining adherents all over the world, and it is also attracting the attention of sports teachers, whose pupils quickly come to regard it as a welcome change to more familiar activities. By combining parkour's varied and natural sequences of moves with more acrobatic elements, a new and as yet uncommon approach to the use of equipment in physical education is evolving. In contrast to the generally standardised moves usually practised in gymnastics, where the emphasis is more on the quality of performance, the stress in parkour is on overcoming obstacles as creatively and effectively as possible, by encouraging pupils to come up with their own solutions. Nevertheless, the example moves presented here are obviously closely related to traditional gymnastics – particularly in the case of vaulting and floor exercises; accordingly, appropriate teaching methods are employed in the lessons as and when appropriate. However, what makes the discipline so attractive is that the practitioner is free to combine moves in any way he sees fit, to achieve a smooth flow of continuous movement. On the level of school sport, a further important advantage is its ability to integrate schoolchildren of all ability levels.

Yet parkour sports are not practised in the same way as classic parkour, freerunning or parcouring. The situation is akin to translating a book from one language to another, with the exception that in this case, the translation is from a familiar, urban environment into a quite foreign one – the school sports hall. As with any translation, this involves a degree of interpretation, which in our case depends on the facilities available and, indeed, is coloured by the way the author's words are understood and interpreted. In particular, the fact that there are so many ways of interpreting the overriding discipline of parkour makes it all the more challenging to find a translation that is acceptable to all participants. Clearly, the reader is free to adopt any or all of the contents, ideals and concepts presented in this book and to rearrange, embellish and develop them as he sees fit. Indeed, I would be very interested to receive any feedback and suggestions that may serve to enrich the teaching potential of these disciplines and stimulate further discussion.

My experience in teaching parkour sports to sixth-form classes is what motivated me to compile this book. The photographs and moves all evolved through teaching regular school students, none of whom had had any prior gymnastics training. All the moves and systematic exercises contained in this book have been tested in practice to verify their suitability. Their success is a clear indication that parkour sports are an eminently appropriate school sports activity, not least due to their obvious kinship with classic gymnastics.

Sascha Rochhausen
Oevenum, August 2009

1. Introduction

1. Origins of parkour

The moves introduced in these sample lessons originate from the disciplines of le parkour, parcouring and freerunning. Since, at their core, all three are based on similar moves, it would make sense to introduce a generic term that integrates them all. However, this should be done in a manner which preserves the identity of the individual disciplines.

The term 'parkour sports' is derived from the most commonly used of the three names, which is itself frequently (albeit often erroneously) used to denote any and all of the aforementioned disciplines.

The term is derived from the French expression 'parcours du combattant', (competition arena), although the discipline is also often known as 'l'Art du Deplacement' (the art of displacement or movement).

Fig. 1: A group of young people practising parkour.

The word 'course' will be used to denote moves or obstacles practised here that are not directly associated with the parkour discipline itself (see the warm-up exercises in the sample lessons).

Parkour was developed in France, and is generally attributed to David Belle and his father Raymond. It was during the Vietnam war that Raymond Belle originally devised a method of movement that could be employed to cross terrain as quickly as possible (this, in turn, was based on the 'Méthode Naturelle' devised by Georges Hébert). Upon his return to France, he taught it to his son, David, and, by the end of the 1980s, the latter had turned the method into a discipline performed in the banlieues, or suburbs, of Paris by a select group of practitioners, who eventually came to refer to themselves as the 'Yamakasi'. As interest grew, David Belle began holding international workshops in the discipline.

As a way of moving through urban terrain, it should not be considered as in any way competitive but as an expression of a way of life, in which any obstacles that may be encountered, such as walls, railings or benches, are overcome as quickly and elegantly as possible; i.e. what may generally be regarded as an obstacle is now no longer seen as such but rather as a minor physical and mental challenge, presented by the need to bridge two points by the shortest possible distance and with a minimum of effort. Ideally, the ensuing movement should evoke a continuous sense of flow (cf. Heinlin 2008).

However, for practitioners of parkour, the discipline is not merely about adopting the most efficient way of moving from one point to another, but also incorporates an element of searching for a new, distinct route, one that is quite unlike any taken by others before. This shows that although often practised in groups, parkour really is a sport for the individual, and also calls into question the frequent claim that the purpose of parkour is not to pitch practitioners against each other in competition. Moreover, the numerous videos in the Internet are themselves evidence of a desire for peer recognition, in that they seek to compare many examples of similar moves in terms of their performance and difficulty.

While parkour concentrates on maximising efficiency in overcoming obstacles, freerunning places the emphasis on elegance, acrobatics and artistic expression. The name most readily associated with freerunning is Sébastien Foucan. He originally trained with David Belle but went on to develop a new understanding of the art, by adding acrobatic elements to the aspect of overcoming obstacles with maximum efficiency.

The third variant is competitive parcouring, which combines moves from both parkour and freerunning. Here, the practitioner (or 'traceur') is required to complete an obstacle course in competition with others. His performance is evaluated in terms of speed and style.

Comparison of parkour sub-disciplines

Parkour	Fast and efficient moves, healthy self-assessment, sense of flow
Freerunning	Acrobatic moves, risk-taking, self-presentation, high level of difficulty
Parcouring	Time pressure, fast, efficient and spectacular moves, competitive basis

From: Heinlin 2008, p. 27.

Parcouring is a discipline of which the founders of parkour disapprove, since it focuses squarely on the aspect of competition, and thus goes against the practice's original philosophy as a lifestyle expression (cf. Hess 2009).

Nowadays, the term parkour is used to denote each of the sub-disciplines, partly because it is the most widespread term and partly because of the lack of a clear understanding of the differences between them.

2. The names of the moves

Since parkour originated in France, many of its moves have French names. However, as the discipline spreads around the world, the original terms are increasingly being replaced by English expressions (both are given in the sample lessons, see ch. 7).

The gracefulness of the discipline's movements has not escaped the attention of the film and advertising industries, and these, in turn, have played an important role in popularising the practice (for example, in the James Bond film "Casino Royal"), raising its status to a 'trend', with its own complement of 'in' terms.

For example, a tucked vault over an obstacle is known as a 'saut de chat' or 'kong vault', and other common moves are the 'speed vault', 'dash vault', 'lazy vault' and 'wall spin'.

However, there is some confusion regarding the terminology, not least caused by the rapid and uncontrolled spread of the various terms through the Internet. As a result, terms are not employed consistently, with both the lazy vault and cat leap often being referred to as a 'saut de chat'. In particular, a single jump often has different names, while identical names are often used to denote different moves.

3. Parkour is varied

An integral feature of parkour is that it employs running to connect moves, resulting in a smooth overall flowing motion, which while giving the discipline its appeal and dynamism, is also one of the main difficulties to be mastered. In this aspect, it is also related to light athletics (e.g. hurdles).

The following moves are fundamental to parkour:

- Running (horizontally and vertically, including pushing off from walls, etc.)
- Balancing (running over railings, etc.)
- Turning (vertically or horizontally, with or without jumping)
- Jumping/vaulting (with or without a support phase, looping)
- Landing (incl. rolling, precise landings on two feet)
- Hanging and swinging (after jumping up onto an obstacle)
- Climbing (on walls, trees, etc.)

The demands placed on the athlete are thus highly varied: in order to move both elegantly and quickly across and over common urban objects, the traceur must display strength, stamina, good technique, good self-estimation, precision, decisiveness, anticipation skills, and creativity.

4. A successful trend

Göring & Lutz (2008) have put together a plausible and succinct summary of the characteristic elements of parkour and the reasons for its success. These are set out in the following (with only minor changes):

1. The practitioner is freed from the temporal and spatial constraints to which most other sports activities are subject. Parkour constitutes individualism in perfection and can be performed virtually anywhere and at any time.

2. Unlike other trend sports, it is not bound to any particular equipment or facilities.

3. The performance aspect of the discipline is regarded by its practitioners as a welcome by-product, resulting from the fact that it tends to be performed at central, populated points.

4. The lack of a competitive factor is compensated for by the challenge presented by particular physical conditions or self-imposed restrictions.

5. Despite the high level of individualism, practitioners often identify with groups, frequently organised through the Internet.

6. Moves are largely learned by trial and imitation. In this way, the individual is his own yardstick and can enjoy the progress and success he attains on his own terms.

5. Parkour sports in school gymnastics

It is virtually impossible to perform parkour with school pupils out of doors, because the local physical environment is generally unaccommodating and there are no safety facilities available. A soft landing is only possible in rare instances, and an error on the street almost always has painful consequences.

However, it is perfectly possible to learn the basic moves of the art in a sports hall equipped with the right facilities, with a wide range of safety methods in place, including mats, safety aids, and spotters. Indeed, traceurs themselves have

recognised these benefits and often use such facilities for training purposes prior to practising moves on the street.

Neither the moves themselves nor the way they are performed are new to sports teaching. Non-standardised, non-competitive gymnastics were developed back in the 1980s, using various equipment combinations and apparatus sequences, and both the aspects of elegance and creativity (also with a partner, see Bruckmann 2000) were emphasised even then (cf. Schmidt-Sinns 2008). Moreover, the standard of the beginners' moves (see ch. 5.1) is comparable with that of the basic forms of school gymnastics, if not easier. Many moves are based on gymnastic skills, and so it only makes sense that parkour, freerunning, and competitive parcouring are now finally finding their way into schools. Parkour therefore presents a perfect opportunity to expand the repertoire of school gymnastics and attract enthusiastic new adherents to the discipline.

However, the incorporation of parkour into school sports activities would appear to harbour at least one contradiction: if parkour has by principle no scoring system, how is it possible to assess pupils' progress? This is an aspect that deserves some attention, especially during the initial phases.

Even if one of the aims of the lessons presented here is to evaluate moves in terms of time and performance, the original principle can still be applied by also incorporating non-assessed elements; indeed the very nature of the activity represents an opportunity to fundamentally rethink the structure of the sports lesson in general (cf. Ide 2007). This is an interesting idea for the sports teacher, who can, if he so chooses, completely dispense with the idea of scoring in parkour activities. This appears perfectly possible bearing in mind that pupils will automatically feel motivated to participate by the very nature of the activity. However, in general it will be found beneficial to introduce some kind of scoring system, in particular if parkour-based activities are to be taught for any length of time. Even if they are not necessarily aware of it, pupils will begin to make their own comparisons as regards their own performance and that of others. Ultimately, it is up to the sports teacher to decide how to proceed on this matter, but this should be done in consultation with the class. It will also depend on the nature of the class itself (e.g. whether it is a school lesson, special interest group, project or sports club activity).

2. Basic Moves

1. Notes on basic moves

This section introduces the basic moves encountered in parkour. Learners must be observed constantly during training and any movement-related deficiencies remedied immediately. Once they have learned to correctly apply the information presented here, participants will know how to avoid body stress imbalances during sustained and intensive training.

Vaults and jumps

Whether performing running jumps or precision jumps, wall runs or gap jumps, and whether jumping off from one foot or both, vaults and jumps are the most common moves performed in parkour.

The sequence of movements for the precision jump is similar to that of the standing long jump, for example. A jump intended to cover a maximum distance should follow the following basic sequence of movements:

Lower the body's centre of gravity and stretch the arms back to add strength to the jump (fig. 2.1). Perform an explosive leg jump making sure to stretch the arms out during take-off (fig. 2.2). In the flight phase, the legs are first tucked up and then stretched far forward (in a 'switchblade' posture), coming to rest on the landing surface with the balls of the feet first (fig. 2.3). Bend the knees strongly upon landing, with arms stretched out forward to maintain balance (fig. 2.4).

Landings

The nature of the landing is inextricably linked with the length and depth of the jump. When jumping from small heights, the front of the foot

Fig. 3: Placing the hands on the floor absorbs the upper body forces when landing from a drop.

comes into contact with the ground first, continuing up to the heel.

This not only applies to landings that follow on from jumps or vaults but is also the natural sequence applied in fast running. This type of landing is recommended when the aim is to absorb all the force incurred in the jump through the feet, e.g. when dropping from small heights or after a running jump (fig. 2.4).

If the forces involved are too great to be absorbed by the feet alone – something which the traceur needs to assess in advance – it will be necessary to lean forward when landing and place the hands on the floor to provide extra support for the upper body (fig. 3). In this case, the feet are not lowered down to the heels, thus maintaining sufficient tension to move the body directly into an upright posture and follow through into a run.

When landing from a great height, a roll will be needed to absorb the majority of the force; a drop or running jump ends by setting down the

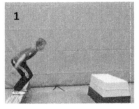   

Fig. 2: Jumps: sequence of movements in the precision jump.

front of the foot, moving directly into a forward lean, with the heels not even coming into contact with the ground. When performing a landing, it is not only necessary to concentrate on foot placement but on the posture of the body as a whole. The knee angle must be no less than 90° upon landing; this protects the knees and allows the forces to be absorbed gradually through the roll.

Quadrupedal movement

This is performed on hands and knees (basic posture), keeping the hands vertically below the shoulders and the toes placed on the floor surface in such a way that the hip and knee both form angles of 90°. The back should be kept straight and the knees prevented from touching the floor. It is important not to look at the hands but to watch the floor ahead of them. Walking on all fours is generally performed by alternately moving one leg and one arm on opposing sides at the same time, being careful not to extend them to the maximum. This allows space for correction to maintain balance. The back should be kept at a constant height when moving (i.e. there should be no upward or downward oscillation). This is controlled through the leg movement, by keeping the knees slightly above the ground.

Balancing

Balancing is highly dependent on form and the quality of performance can vary rapidly. It is very important to maintain a positive demeanour. Simply adopting a serious intention to master a particular course can have a decisive impact on the quality of performance.

When balancing, the heel and front foot around the second toe should be kept in contact with the beam, to ensure the greatest possible area of contact. If the foot contact concentrates around the big toe, the contact area will be diminished and the ability to maintain control will suffer accordingly.

It is important to concentrate the gaze ahead of the feet and not at the feet themselves. The knees should be slightly bent, to allow any mistakes to be corrected. If the body is fully outstretched, only the arms will be available to perform any compensatory movements.

Fig. 5: Balancing: concentrate on the area ahead of the feet.

Fig. 4: Quadrupedal movement: knees move parallel to the floor.

Fig. 6: Balancing: keep knees slightly bent.

2. Descriptions of moves and variations

The moves presented here are based on the ones most commonly performed in parkour, freerunning and competitive parcouring, and should therefore be regarded as model movements. Nevertheless, when a movement is presented in one of the lessons, the description should not be taken as binding or standardised. On the contrary, the moves lend themselves to a wide range of variation, a fact borne out by observation. This is due to the aspect of efficiency. Since environmental conditions vary greatly, it makes sense for the traceur to modify his movements to fit in with the immediate physical scenario. This means that under certain circumstances, rather than sticking to a strict sequence of steps, it may make sense to perform a particular move in a way that differs from the model movement described here.

It is important that the practitioner gradually learns to vary his moves out of doors, where conditions can vary constantly. Parkour adherents have come to realise that the best way of overcoming an obstacle involves employing a minimum of bodily resources, so as to conserve strength and energy. However, movement variations also have their place in a sports hall environment. Not only do physical constitutions vary from person to person but so does an individual's personal form, sometimes even on a daily basis, as does his ability to assess an obstacle. There are therefore many reasons why it can make sense to amend a given movement. A different run-up to an obstacle or an unsuccessful take-off may also necessitate a deviation from the model movements, to restore a move's efficiency and safety.

This is illustrated by the following example variations.

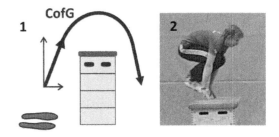

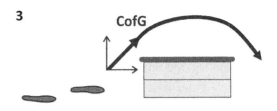

Fig. 8: From an almost centric (top) to an extremely eccentric force action (bottom); the kong vault can be varied by amending the take-off movement.

Example 1: Kong vault
The kong vault (see 7.2) and split-foot kong vault (see 7.1-3) are both related to the tucked jump, but they differ considerably from each other in terms of their take-off. The simple kong vault is performed at high force with both legs together, making it suitable for higher, shorter obstacles, since the body's centre of gravity (CofG) at the moment of take-off is above the feet and acceleration is almost vertical (virtually centric) (ills. 8.1-2). In the split-foot kong vault, (fig. 8.3: split-foot), the body's centre of gravity is above the front

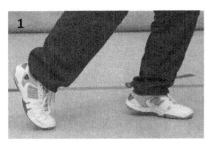

Fig. 7: Movement variation: split-foot kong vault.

Fig. 9: Reverse vault: vertical take-off from both feet.

Fig. 10: Reverse vault: single-footed take-off (scissor position) with horizontal trajectory.

foot, and an eccentric burst of force is exerted on it. The rotational movement about the centre of gravity pulls the legs strongly upward and causes the upper body to lean far forward with the hands reaching right out. The split-foot kong vault is therefore primarily suited to low, wide obstacles.

Example 2: Reverse vault

There are a number of ways of varying the reverse vault (see ch. 7.3). First of all, the traceur can place either one or both hands on the obstacle for support (beginners, in particular, often feel that using both hands is simpler and safer). The choice of whether to use one or two arms for support has little impact on the efficiency of the move. It is merely a question of difficulty and both variations can form part of a methodical teaching programme.

The second variation concerns the movement of the legs over the obstacle: either the vault commences from both feet, tucking up and closing the legs in the flight phase (fig. 9), or from one foot (scissor position, fig. 10), with legs open, resulting in a flatter trajectory followed by a landing in a step position. Although the second variation appears the more efficient, the angular velocity is lower since the mass is further away from the pivot (support arm). In practice, though, the differences in speed are negligible, and both

variations can be regarded as valuable moves in parkour sports. Deciding which move is more appropriate has more to do with the nature of the obstacle itself – if it is low and wide, the one-legged take-off is the more efficient – if not the only – choice, as it involves a low and wide trajectory over the obstacle. However, if the obstacle is narrow and high, a double-footed, almost vertical take-off is required, and the subsequent tucking in of the legs can be accompanied by a fast turn.

Example 3: Speed vault

The speed vault (ch. 7.2) can also be varied by the way the hands are used for support (fig. 12): Using one arm for permanent support in overcoming the obstacle is already efficient, but extra propulsion can be obtained, if necessitated by the dimensions of the obstacle, by additionally pushing off from the other hand a moment later (fig. 11).

The important factor here is not only efficiency, but also effectiveness, i.e. the employment of a particular variant movement to enable the objective to be reached in the first place.

Example 4: Dash vault

The dash vault (ch. 7.4) can be performed either with a frontal run-up and simultaneous two-arm support phase or with staggered two-arm support (fig. 13). This variation results primarily from

Fig. 11: Speed vault with two-handed support for added push-off propulsion.

the angle of run-up. If approaching the obstacle from an angle, one arm will reach it before the other one, in which case it only makes sense (and it is only possible) to use this arm before applying the other one. Since there are certain situations in which an angled approach is beneficial, and a frontal run-up indeed impossible, this variant move is sometimes essential.

The need to vary moves results from the fact that obstacles, external conditions, current form, and physical fitness vary from person to person and also change in line with an individual's cur-

rent constitution. This is particularly important when moves are performed out of doors and not in a gymnasium or sports hall equipped with uniform facilities. Variation evolves naturally when pupils of differing abilities seek to overcome an obstacle using the same model move. Clearly, in parkour sports, such variations should not be regarded as in any way wrong; indeed they are desirable, in that they conform fully with the concept of freedom of thought and movement. One of the intrinsic features of parkour is that its practitioners constantly adapt their moves and behaviour

Fig. 12: Speed vault with single-hand support phase.

both to the current environment and their individual ability, without subjecting themselves to any regulations or standards.

Another important factor is that when overcoming an obstacle, each pupil is free to select what he considers to be the safest means of doing so; this means that, if need be, the aspect of movement control stands above the aspect of efficiency. This focus should be maintained consistently in all school-based activities. It is therefore essential for the teacher to equip pupils with as many variations as possible when teaching model movements, to maximise the scope for learning (e.g. employing different equipment heights, lengths, etc.). The pupils of a group should not be given one single obstacle for them all to practice with, but a selection of obstacles with various heights and lengths, to accommodate pupils' different ability levels and to point out the importance of variant movements.

No kind of scoring should be employed with the move, since this would mean (unconsciously) risking introducing standardisation, which would hinder pupils in discovering their own creative, fast and flowing solution to an obstacle and exercising their own individual interpretation of a situation.

On the other hand, parkour should not be allowed to lead to a situation of complete arbitrariness. Boundaries in parkour are found in personal ability levels, reflected by varying levels of confidence, fluidity of movement, and the taking of unnecessary risks. Whenever a person attempts to exceed his own abilities, he not only puts himself at risk but also violates one of the most important principles of the discipline: "learn to gauge yourself and do not overestimate your ability!" Nevertheless, the need for a variant move

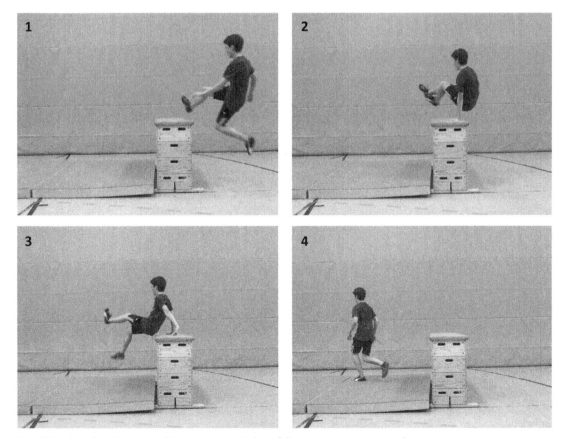

Fig. 13: Dash vault with staggered two-arm support phase following a run-up at an angle.

should always be questioned, to determine its usefulness:

"What is it that makes this change or variation to a move's performance easier, faster or safer compared with the model move"?

> The motto for parkour could then be: Whatever a practitioner considers to be *safe, efficient and effective* in accomplishing a movement can be said to be "correct" for him.

3. Discussion

1. Philosophy

On the surface, the various parkour disciplines appear to consist solely of their physical elements. From an outsider's point-of-view, there is little evidence that for many traceurs, physical activity is merely the visible expression of an underlying state of mind, which is actually part of a core philosophy adhered to by many who practice the discipline. While freerunning has a less comprehensive or intensely discussed philosophy, for parkour's core adherents it is just as important to live according to the underlying philosophy as it is to uphold the precepts of effective and efficient movement.

The ideals pursued by freerunners are succinctly expressed by Edwardes (2009, p. 10), in the chapter entitled 'A new idealism', as:

> "...a discipline founded on pushing their limits and seeking a way to reach anywhere they choose to go, no matter how difficult the path."

Although this is not in itself a fundamental contradiction of the ideals of parkour, according to one of its most famous proponents from the Parkour Generations group, the discipline is rooted in the conscious expansion of one's limits, achieved first and foremost by engaging in a constant search for physical challenge.

In parkour, on the other hand, the ideals are more complex and holistic in nature, in that its practitioners do not regard the discipline merely as a sporting activity but as an attitude to life, central aspects of which include safety, sustainability and efficiency (Luksch 2009). The foremost requirement is discipline. Even if the ideals are not laid down in any kind of codex, there is no doubt that self-promotion, unnecessary risk taking, and commercialism are strictly rejected, while a healthy diet, the rejection of drugs, and respect for the environment and one's fellow man constitute central principles. Clearly, any situation will require a holistic modification of movement, behaviour and spirit, for which reason the uniformisation of movement is generally avoided within the parkour community. Although they too support and desire the search for physical challenge and the expansion of personal limits, the focal point of their activity is always to move in harmony with the environment and not simply to enact some kind of performance spectacle.

The following principles have come to enjoy consicerable respect among parkour practitioners:

Prevention

Many injuries can be avoided by commencing training sessions with an intensive general warm-up and conditioning session (which can also be repeated during the training).

Mental strength

The aim is to improve one's physical performance and skill at one's own speed, without being subject to persuasion or risk taking. Particularly when training in groups, this means not only having to but also being able to say 'No' to a challenge, when required. While traceurs should never try and exert pressure on others, what is perhaps more difficult is learning to cope with one's own expectations and goals. A traceur can test his ability in this regard by critically asking himself in difficult situations if he is in full control of the situation and able to act in the manner required of him. In the end, positive thinking will open up paths and possibilities of overcoming situations and transcending limitations.

Health

The frequent repetition of movements demands varied training and gentle forms of (anatomically balanced) exertion.

For example, stress to the joints should be minimised by practising soft and quiet landings. Body signals should not be ignored, and training should immediately be halted if the participant is in any pain. Every individual is called upon to show responsibility for himself.

At first glance, the philosophy may appear of

secondary importance when the discipline is practised within a school setting, but it is still important for the teacher to appreciate what makes parkour different if he wishes to enjoy the acceptance of all the pupils, particularly those who are already adherents of the discipline's ideals. This is evidenced by the discussions in Internet forums in which superficial parkour teaching comes in for some criticism. Teachers can avoid this by ensuring that the backgrounds to the various disciplines enjoy adequate explanation, if possible given by pupils themselves, whose motivation should then be taken seriously.

If pupils then accept the ideals of parkour, it can only serve to help them in their personal development, as all of the ideals embody positive personality characteristics.

2. The term 'parkour sports'

This book deals with parkour sports – but why do we need a new term?

The numerous depictions and descriptions of parkour and freerunning, particularly in the Internet, show clearly that although the boundaries between the disciplines are (meanwhile) generally well known, the distinction between them is increasingly – and consciously – blurred, leading to uncertainty as to what constitutes either the one or the other. This is also evidenced by the fact that the broad public tends to concentrate less on practising parkour on a purist level and more on combining moves with turns and jumps which traditional parkour adherents would consider as ineffective or inefficient with regard to the obstacle or situation to be overcome. Nevertheless, the term 'parkour' still tends to be preferred to 'freerunning', although occasionally both are used (see various book titles). One reason for this is that traceurs often use 'inefficient' moves in training to expand their repertoire of moves, the result of which, once mastered, they regard as an improvement in their personal efficiency, attained while adhering to the precepts of parkour (or wishing to do so).

For this reason, there are some practitioners who have begun using the alternative term of 'my parkour', which shows that the interpretation of the philosophy has been expanded and so the content of the moves now consciously deviates from their original forms. Hence the aspect of individualisation is being driven on along with (or even because of) the increasing spread and development of the discipline.

In the context of school sport, in which a free choice of moves from any of the disciplines is permitted, parkour sports is an appropriate collective term with which the (original) identity of the individual disciplines can still be preserved without accidentally blurring their distinctions or ignoring their differences. This can be done by ensuring that both the backgrounds (ch. 3.1: Philosophy) and the affiliations of the various disciplines – as identified in the sample lessons – are also covered in the classes.

3. The transfer problem

The origins of both parkour and freerunning are in outdoor urban terrain, and naturally, this remains the place where they should continue to be practised. The urban landscape presents the traceur with a constant challenge of new obstacles to overcome, demanding great concentration and flexibility, not to mention a wide repertoire of moves. However when practising with standardised equipment, these factors are after a while, no longer so stringently required.

On the other hand, what hall training does constitute, on the other hand, is a safe training environment in which to practice coordination skills and simulate particularly unusual moves. They are then easier – not to mention safer – to employ in the street, and the practitioner will have added to his repertoire while minimising the risk factor.

This is not to suggest that it is always possible to transfer moves directly and unreservedly from the hall to the street, since conditions in a real urban landscape, such as the hardness and roughness of materials and unevenness of terrain, can vary greatly, and weather conditions can affect levels of visibility and surface moisture (i.e. grip). As a result, previously learned moves often have to be varied or other moves substituted. For example, if a surface is moist or rough, more care must be taken when using the hands for support, necessitating a shorter distance in which to overcome the obstacle.

Example: The roll

Performing a roll outdoors on paving stones, tarmac or even rougher outdoor terrain, in the absence of a soft surface such as a mat, is immediately uncomfortable and unpleasant. As a consequence, practitioners will prefer to employ softer, fleshier parts of the body (cf. Luksch 2009). Depending on the characteristics of the back muscles, the way in which a roll is performed may be amended by directing it more towards the side, relative to the direction of movement, with the back barely rounded at all (see marking in fig. 14.3). This avoids the shoulder blade and vertebral extensions coming into painful contact with the ground. It is therefore up to the traceur himself to find out, by frequent practice, how best

Fig. 15: Parkour in an urban scenario: the roll performed diagonally over the shoulder.

to fashion a movement in accordance with his particular physical characteristics. Of course, this can also be practised on the floor of the sports hall, but it is not advisable to do this with schoolchildren and in any case, it is likely to be rejected by many pupils, citing the example of the forward roll. While a hard floor presents little scope for performing a roll without pain, using a soft mat allows for considerable variation without the risk of discomfort. It is even possible to employ movements that resemble a forward roll, which on a hard surface would almost certainly be painful.

Fig. 14: Performing a roll without pain or injury on the hard surface of a sports hall floor.

Easy to feel...

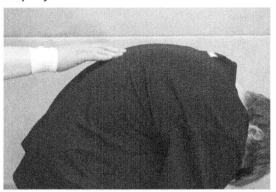

Fig. 16: When the back is rounded, the bones can be clearly felt (here the spiny dendrites of the vertebrae).

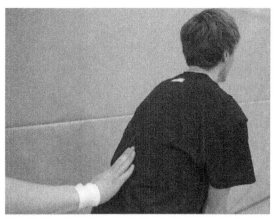

Fig. 17: Resolving the rounded back: the bones hardly protrude and the longitudinal back muscles now form the highest protrusions.

This could result in a false sense of security when leaving the safe environment of the hall and attempting to perform a supposedly safe move on the road. In general, in the extensive absence of safety zones and outside assistance, it is necessary to employ lower altitudes and distances when practising on the real world. In expectation of pupils' desire to experiment with moves in the street, the teacher should ensure that this theme is adequately covered during lessons. Moreover, the most sustainable training effect is attained by aiming for gradual improvement through frequent repetition, even with moves requiring more skill.

Summary: "When practising on the street, start again (and again) from the beginning and increase your skill gradually!"

Fig. 18: Performing a roll on a concrete surface.

Fig. 19: The rolling movement on a soft surface with a more rounded back, progressing in the direction of movement.

4. The case for parkour sports

The many articles and books that have been written recently on the subject of parkour and freerunning, not to mention the great amount of feedback received by the author of this book, are evidence of the growing level of interest in these disciplines among sports teachers (and, in the experience of teachers, among pupils too). School pupils show particular enthusiasm when practising parkour sports and can often be seen encouraging each other to attain their personal best performances, frequently showing little envy in their recognition of each other's abilities. Parkour sports represent a modern approach to sports teaching in that they accommodate individual pupils' interests and allow for open-ended exercises.

The discipline's value in sports teaching, from an educational point of view too, lies in its flexible nature, and it is this that makes it so attractive to a large number of pupils. It appears to fulfil its overriding aim of motivating pupils to undertake more physical movement in their leisure time.

The benefits of teaching parkour in sports classes can be summed up as follows:

- By allowing the free selection of the method used to overcome an obstacle, all participants experience a sense of achievement.
- Physical demands can be gradually intensified to allow personal improvements in performance to be easily gauged.
- For pupils, the focus is on discernable goals, such as safety, efficiency and self-evaluation.
- The individual exercises all relate to each other within a common context: they are moves that are adapted to fit the immediate environment.
- The general aim of moving fluidly through an obstacle landscape is frequently achieved intuitively and is motivational.
- Many pupils' interests can be accommodated by paying attention to the selection of apparatus, basic moves, evaluation criteria and discipline orientation.
- Teachers can conduct a variable evaluation of pupils' abilities, taking into account individual skill levels.
- Assessment focuses less on comparison with others and more on personal betterment, combined with identifying individual limits.
- Athletic factors can be combined with aesthetic aspects or they can be employed independently of each other.
- The majority of moves lend themselves well to variation.

All in all, personal success is not necessarily concerned with possessing certain physical traits. This is an important factor, because in traditional school gymnastics – in contrast to parkour – fewer and fewer pupils are able to match the increasing demand of the exercises, and unsurprisingly, their motivation drops as a consequence of their minimal expectation of success. Parkour sports restore the fun element by allowing pupils to develop moves gradually and gently, and providing easy to learn movements, such as those presented here, which facilitate newcomers in particular to gain a feel for the discipline. By experiencing the resultant success, pupils are motivated into familiarising themselves with more demanding gymnastic moves (such as flips and loops).

By accommodating parkour moves into school gymnastics teaching, it is possible to place the aspect of promoting talent in the field of gymnastics on a broader basis.

4. Teaching Methodology

1. Teaching time

The sample lessons are based on a teaching time of 90 minutes (i.e. a double period) and have been tested on this basis. Since the discipline makes considerable use of gymnastics equipment, single-period lessons are not advisable. Every lesson should include warm-up and relaxation phases. The game phase is conceived as a motivational module and forms an integral part of each sample lesson. It may be dispensed with if there is a lack of time and the theme of the lesson and the exercises are particularly demanding (see advice in: Suggested games 7.10/7.11). It is also possible to divide the sample lessons into two parts, particularly if they cover a double theme (see ch. 7.1/7.4/7.8/7.12).

The lessons are conceived to be conducted over an extended period of time. It is possible to pick out individual lessons but to do so would mean losing out on one important goal – that of promoting the pupils' ability to evaluate their own skills.

2. Location

The ideal hall dimensions correspond to the size of two volleyball courts. This would allow the introductory running exercises and warm-up courses to be conducted alongside each other and would also allow several small groups to perform different exercises alongside each other at the same time. This is of particular advantage when a wide range of abilities have to be accommodated within a single group, where weaker pupils, intimidated by the more spectacular achievements of the better ones, would tend to remain in the background if all participants practised together.

If only a small space is available (at least the area of one volleyball court), this is quite sufficient; however, it will be necessary to set up the various equipment stages closer together or to employ fewer variations.

3. Safety

The risk potential involved in parkour exercises is comparable to that of regular gymnastics, and can be considered low, provided certain safety measures are adhered to. A common criticism concerns the risk involved by dropping from a height, as this places considerable strain on the joints. For this reason, it is very important to place sufficient emphasis on the roll as described here (ch. 7.6), as a method of absorbing energy. Similarly, it is just as important to avoid excessive dropping heights (in excess of a person's reach). Safety facilities, including landing mats and spotters, must be constantly available to those performing the exercises. Criticism can be countered by pointing out that dismounting from hoops and horizontal bars in regular gymnastics also involves jumping from similar heights.

Pupils should develop a sense of routine in the provision of safety assistance. Precise explanations of the assistance to be given will be dispensed with here (with the exception of the wall flip). Commonly practised standard measures and spotter techniques apply (see Becker et al., 1998; Gerling, 2006). All safety facilities – mats, equipment, etc. – are to be employed as shown.

Fig. 20: Spotters clasp the upper arms in a reverse arm grip for the backward wall flip.

4. Exercises

When an exercise consists of a number of steps, the image sequences are numbered. Unnumbered pictures illustrate an exercise in its entirety.

The exercises should be regarded as a collection of suggestions. Applied in the given sequence, they comprise the method to be employed for performing the relevant move. Individual exercises can be left out if required, if time doesn't allow or pupils already have the necessary ability. In general, however, it is recommended that exercises are performed in the given order during the lesson and the apparatus is left assembled to allow time for individual practice. In any case, it can be assumed that not every pupil will be able to perform every exercise and that the time they need for each one will vary greatly (see 5. Differentiation). The teacher must ensure that appropriate safety measures (for example, a trained spotter) are in place at each equipment stage which they are not themselves able to supervise in the course of a lesson.

5. Differentiation

The sample lessons were conceived as elements of a sixth-form elective course, but certain exercises, modified appropriately, can also be employed at lower senior or even junior levels (e.g. simple jumps, climbing, etc.).

Fig. 21: Different apparatus heights set for the precision jump.

If at all possible, apparatus should be set up for pupils of all abilities, to enable weaker pupils to participate while still allowing stronger ones to feel challenged. The nature of the exercise courses is determined by the teacher and the pupils together and modified in the course of the lesson. In most cases, this process will take care of

itself, since the necessary variations to the apparatus will present themselves automatically (e.g. raising boxes, increasing distances, dismantling equipment aids, etc.). The teacher is called upon here to point out limitations and dictate safety aspects. The teacher is also responsible for detecting any overadventurously constructed apparatus (unstable boxes, course sections with no safety provision, etc.) and to correct them or prevent them being used.

The apparatus constructions shown in the illustrations are intended as a guide only, as are the heights indicated in the exercises. It is recommended that exercises begin at a low height, to suit the age group, performance levels and body sizes of the pupils.

6. Promoting independence

Although the sample lessons already include introductory running exercises, warm-up courses and relaxation phases, this section of the lesson can be left in the hands of the pupils. The author has made considerable positive experience in asking two different pupils to prepare the warm-up programme for each lesson (this stage can also be used for assessment purposes). This not only teaches pupils the necessity of warm-up exercises but it also allows them to familiarise themselves with the effect they have on the body and enables them to expand the exercises.

It is recommended, however, that the teacher leads the warm-up and relaxation exercises in the first few lessons, before subsequently leaving them up to the pupils. It will only take a few lessons for the pupils to organise themselves (for further information, see: www.parkoursport.com -> Materials).

7. Parkour exercises in large groups

It is always particularly challenging for a sports teacher to teach apparatus-intensive activities such as parkour to a large group. Frequently, the success of such activities is down to the factor of organisation. Hence, the teaching of parkour sports requires thorough planning of the various equipment stages, which, of course, includes ensuring the availability of the apparatus, and fast reconfiguration of equipment, whenever this is required. A good approach is to assemble an exercise stage at a fixed position, which can then be adapted into any new context presenting itself in the course of the lesson, without itself undergo-ing any major changes.

The individual stages in each lesson should generally be constructed completely to minimise the interruptions to the flow of both lesson and movement caused by reassembling equipment.

If appropriate, stages may also be incorporated from previous lessons, to intensify the effect of the exercise phases overall, to allow any pupils who missed the previous lesson to catch up, and to include an equipment stage that can be used by several small groups.

As a result, the group divides up among the various stages in accordance with their learning

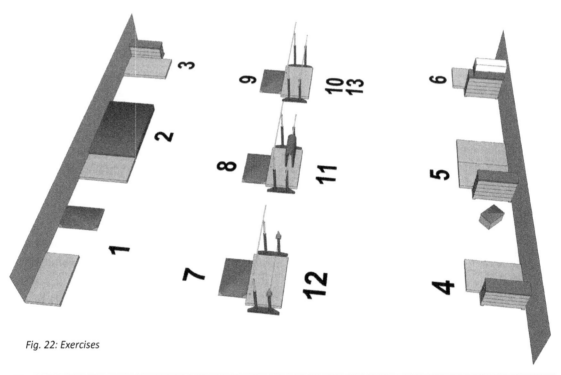

Fig. 22: Exercises

Stage	Explanation
1 - 6	Wall run over obstacles of gradually increasing lengths and heights.
7 - 9	Underbar following run-up to the asymmetrical bars from behind, and dismount over the lower bar.
10	Spiral underbar: squat on the lower bar and dismount.
11	Spiral underbar: pass over the mat.
12	Spiral underbar: run up and swing over the rubber cord.
13	Spiral underbar: perform target move.

speed, in turn increasing the active time for each pupil.

8. Example of organising equipment

The following instructions for Lesson Five (see ch. 7.5) are given as an example of how to organise equipment. The numbers in the illustrations indicate the order in which they are used (see fig. 22). All the stages in this sample lesson are combined in the concluding game (see fig. 23).

At the beginning of the lesson (following the warm-up phase), the wall run is set up in a quickly organised sequence from a previous lesson (stages 1-6). The underbar moves practised in a previous lesson are then performed (stages 7-9). These are easy to perform and prepare pupils for the ensuing intensive arm work that the target move itself involves. Finally, stages 10-13 are performed as a methodical sequence for teaching spiral underbars (see ch. 7.5 for explanations).

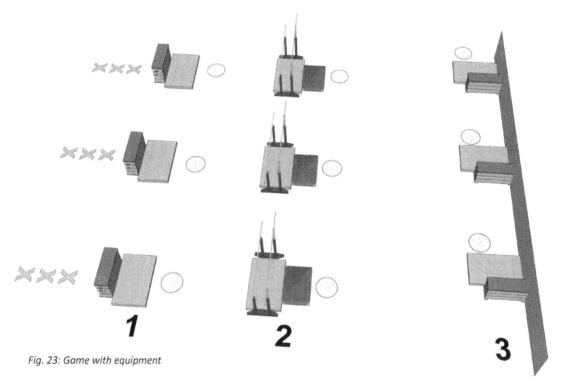

Fig. 23: Game with equipment

Stage	Explanation
1	Vault over box with freely selected jump.
2	Perform spiral underbars on asymmetric bars.
3	Overcome three-tier box with wall run.

Rules of the game

Two obstacle courses, each consisting of three obstacle combinations, are set up using the equipment assembled previously. For each group, three exercise hoops are laid out after each obstacle, each containing a certain number of objects (e.g. tennis balls). Each player from a team may pick up only one ball per run. It is up to either the group or the individual player to decide which hoop to run to. The object of the game is to bring back all the balls to the group as quickly as possible. The aim is also to promote self-evaluation by teaching the runners to recognise which hoop each runner should run to bearing in mind his abilities, thus ensuring a good overall group result. The tactical aspect may well have an effect on who wins the game.

Once the exercises have been performed, the stages are rearranged in accordance with the game plan (fig. 23). In this example, the group is divided into three teams. This may, however, be amended in line with the available equipment.

5. Sequence of Activities in a Typical Sample Lesson

1. Warm-up

Each lesson begins with a general warm-up round, comprising a few simple running exercises. If you also wish to include games at this stage, they should not be too demanding either in terms of organisation or exertion. Subsequent exercises should build gradually, culminating in the concluding game, that should always form the highlight of the session. It should be borne in mind that games played in warm-up activities harbour an increased injury potential, as the body is not attuned to performing intense physical activity at this stage.

Pupils should become accustomed to this phase of the activities early on, as it is essential in preparing the body for physical performance.

Fig. 24: Warm-up exercise comprising running.

The general running exercises are followed by a second warm-up phase, consisting of an exercise course for coordination and improving stamina. Both construction and dismantling of the exercise courses are a group activity. Around 15 minutes should be allowed for the warm-up phase as a whole. This should be sufficient for setting up, imparting the requisite instructions, and conducting about three run-throughs per person.

The warm-up phase should address the requirements of speed, agility, stamina, extended exertion, and coordination (itself comprising several skills: orientation, reaction, combination, reconfiguration, differentiation, balancing, and rhythm), i.e. all the general skills which are required for performing parkour sports. The majority of stages involve running, which places the emphasis on continuity and developing stamina, and minimises breaks during phases of intense activity.

Although the various stages should be undertaken at speed, it is more important to ensure that exercises are performed correctly. To maintain a rapid throughput, individual stages should only be repeated if really necessary. If required, an additional course can be constructed from cones, to minimise waiting times. After completing the course, participants should conclude the activity by running around the hall a set number of times.

A tennis ball can be used as an 'entrance ticket' to prevent too many people from accumulating at a particular exercise stage. With five to six stages, one tennis ball between six to eight participants has been found to be appropriate. This also prevents people from commencing too rapidly one after the other, because a runner is only permitted to hand over his ball once he has reached his target, and only then can the next runner begin. With some stages, the ball can also be incorporated in the exercise.

Exercise stages that constitute a higher level of effort should be constructed several times in parallel (in the diagrams, each stage is only illustrated once, to maintain clarity). For some stages, a number is given in brackets (see ch. 7.1: Warm-up course); this should be regarded as a suggestion for the optimum number of such stages.

There should always be an instructor available at stages that are somewhat more difficult, or where equipment may move out of place or constitute a hazard. This person is responsible for giving direct feedback or assistance and correcting errors. Since this may be difficult to organise, all sample lessons contain no more than one such 'critical exercise', to simplify organisation and allow the teacher to maintain supervision over the class. When a lesson contains such an exercise, it is indicated in the instructions by the symbol: *. (e.g. ch. 7.1: Warm-up course).

The author regards is it as important that individual courses address a variety of exercise requirements. However, coordination exercises are specifically employed to prevent the risk of premature exhaustion in the warm-up phase.

Fig. 25: Warm-up course conceived to promote fitness.

Variety can be introduced by employing 1-4 different stages and instructing pupils to change every so often. For some courses, this may also serve to increase the active exercise time. All courses can be altered in this way. Apparatus 7.9 is an example of this kind of activity.

To promote cooperation, individual courses can be performed in pairs. It is also possible to construct exercise stages that can only be completed with a partner, perhaps in hand contact or simultaneously (see ch. 7.14: Warm-up course). To promote trust, a course can be set up in such a way that it can be performed blindfold (see ch. 7.3: Warm-up course), with one partner guiding the other through the course, either by hand or using a rope.

Another variation is for small groups to move from one course to the next in no fixed order (all warm-up courses can be performed in this way). The teacher gives a signal to change after a certain amount of time or a certain number of repetitions. It will be necessary to decide beforehand if the participants are to move on individually or as a group.

The distances in the courses are oriented to-wards the dimensions of a volleyball pitch (9m x 18m). These distances evolve naturally according to the size of the apparatus and the appropriate path lengths leading from one equipment stage to the next.

2. Main training

The main training exercises (see headings in the sample lessons) form the core learning materials of the lesson, and as such are performed following the warm-up and before the final game. The suggested sequence is to arrange the main items in order of increasing difficulty. Since almost every lesson is in itself a coherent unit, the order can be altered or shortened, if this suits the purpose of the lesson. This applies in particular to lessons covering moves primarily associated with freerunning (indicated as such in the lesson), as they do not represent a move required for overcoming an obstacle. The sequence is, therefore, not binding, and should be modified to suit the pupils' level of ability and the available time. It should, however, also be pointed out that freerunning moves tend to be highly motivational.

The main training sessions comprise sequences of moves of increasing difficulty, which gradually approach the level of the target move. In consistence with the original principles of parkour, it is important that the moves taught in the lessons are not regarded as binding or standardised. The performance of the move should be modified to the respective obstacle, which may necessitate deviating from the moves shown.

3. Concluding game

Each sample lesson concludes with a game based on the apparatus. The aim of this is to give pupils an opportunity to apply what they have learned, and to enhance the general enjoyment level. It is also an opportunity to integrate participants by incorporating their suggestions and deciding how to ensure safe play and maximum enjoyment.

Chapter 8 contains an overview of all equip-

Fig. 26: Cat leap from an apparatus combination.

Fig. 27: Yoga exercises for relaxation.

ment games. Each sample lesson contains a reference to a game.

4. Agility training and relaxation

The relaxation phase allows participants to wind down from the exertion of the main exercise. It gives pupils a chance to gather themselves, consciously relax the body and, where appropriate, to look back over the events of the session. Activities can include stand-up stretch exercises, yoga or pilates, massage, or an imagined journey. This should always be seen as a fixed element with sufficient variety to maintain enjoyment.

The following guidelines apply to stretching and agility activities:

1. Exercises should always be performed slowly and uniformly.
2. Go into the stretch slowly, holding the position of greatest stretch for 5-10 minutes.
3. Exit the stretch slowly; repeat three to four times.
4. Breath calmly and uniformly, and never hold the breath (danger of forced respiration: an undersupply of oxygen leads to a cramped posture).
5. Stretch all groups of muscles if possible.
6. Loosen up after each exercise.
7. As far as possible, do not incorporate more than five stretch exercises in a programme of activities.

A choice of stretch and relaxation exercises is given in ch. 9, from which the teacher can select as appropriate. The first five sample lessons already contain a choice of exercises.

6. Illustrations and Symbols

1. List of gymnastics apparatus

Equipment	Illustration	Equipment	Illustration
Small box		Tennis ball, half tennis balls	
Large box (3-5 sections)		Balance bar	
Gymnastics mat		Medicine ball	
Crash mat		Softball	
Pole and stand		Ceiling rope	
Bench		Springboard	
Skipping rope (2-3 m)		Carpet tile	
Hoop		Cone	
Stopwatch		Horse/buck	
Asymmetric bars		Wall bars	
Horizontal bar and landing mat		Landing mat	
Parallel bars			

2. Symbols and abbreviations

X	Player/performer
O	Opponent
P	Number of persons
CofG	Body's centre of gravity

 Parkour (or parcouring) element

 Freerunning element

 Circle/oval exercise

 Running exercise, there and back

 Exercise with crossing paths

⟶ Paths

 On-the-spot exercises

Additional materials are available from the Internet, at:

www.parkoursport.com/materials.php

Material updates are published on a regular basis. These comprise assembly diagrams for the equipment stages used in each lesson, some with suggestions for variant assemblies, plus additional equipment courses for use in warm-up exercises, a warm-up guide, and scoring suggestions for use with timed exercises.

7. Sample Lessons

Lesson 1   Balancing and Precision Jumps

Introduction

An extended course programme in parkour training should begin with balancing and precision jumping exercises; these are important as they constitute some of the most basic moves used in parkour sports. Teachers can expect the exercises outlined below to be within the reach of all pupils, hence their suitability as introductory exercises. The balancing exercises are not based on any specific movements and they can be developed as necessary to suit the needs of the class.

For this reason, the moves that comprise this lesson are presented in no particular methodical order.

1. Warm-up

No.	Activity		P	Materials	Illustration
Running exercise					
1	Run one circuit, to loosen up.	⟳	1	-	
2	When instructed to do so, run one circuit sprinting, taking short, fast steps (for 5 seconds).	⟳	1	-	
3	Then run one circuit touching the lines on the floor, followed each time by a complete turn about the body's longitudinal axis.	⟳	1	-	

Warm-up course: See end of lesson: Warm-up course - Assembly 1

2. 1. Balance – Équilibre

Materials: Benches, medicine balls, box sections, horizontal bars, skipping rope, landing mats, asymmetrical bars, small boxes, large boxes.

Exercises

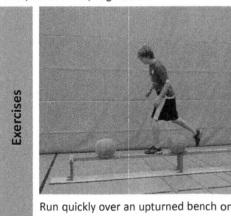

Run quickly over an upturned bench on which medicine balls have been placed.

Foot fight on an upturned bench.

1. Balance along the edges of a detached box section.

2. Upon reaching the end of the box section, turn around without stepping off.

Walk over upturned benches and medicine balls.

Walk over a combination of upturned bench, medicine balls, and box sections.

Balance along a horizontal bar.

Skip along an upturned bench.

Balance along both parallel bars on all fours.

Place box sections of increasing height at either end of the parallel bars: Balance along both bars in an upright position.

Exercises

45

Balance along one bar on all fours (cat balancing).

Balance along a horizontal bar while leaning frontally onto a wall.

2. 2. Precision jump – Saut de précision

Materials: horizontal bar set at knee height with landing mats at far end, and two small boxes at front of bar, set 50 centimetres one behind the other.

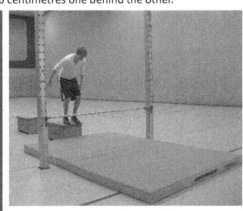

1. Perform a two-legged take-off from the small box using the arms to support the swing.

2. Land with balls of feet on the knee-high horizontal bar, maintaining stability atop the bar.

Materials: benches, landing mats, asymmetrical bars, large boxes.

1. Power exercise: stand on tiptoes on the edge of a bench.

2. Alternately push up and come back down, keeping legs stretched.

1. Perform a two-legged take-off from one box.

2. Land on lower bar while simultaneously gripping the upper bar.

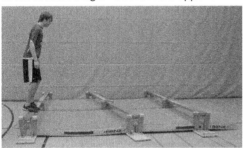

3. Dismount: swing off beneath the upper bar...

3. ... or do a turn vault over the upper bar.

1. Jump from one upturned bench to the next.

2. Vary the spaces between the benches by orienting the middle bench diagonally.

1. Jump from an upturned bench onto a box.

2. Note: Do not attempt to jump in the other direction as there is a high risk of injuring joints!

3. **Suggested games:** Throw-off (see Game 1)

4. **Relaxation:** See ch. 9, exercises 20, 29, 32, 33, 38

Exercises

Warm-up course **Assembly 1**

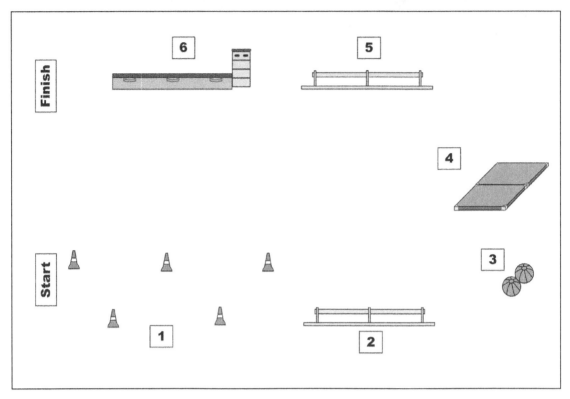

Number	Materials	Number	Materials	Number	Materials
5	Cones	2	Benches	2	Medicine balls
2	Gymnastics mats	1	Large box	1	Crash mat

Stage	Object of exercise	Explanation
Start		Participants pass through the course individually, progressing from start to finish.
1	Coordination	Run sideways around cones placed far apart.
2 *	Coordination	Run over an upturned bench, halting several times and touching the bench with the knees, before standing up and moving into a tiptoe position.
3 (2)	Power endurance	Sit against the wall: holding a medicine ball, stretch the arms forward and throw the ball over your head onto the wall. Then catch the medicine ball. Alternatively, use a volleyball.
4	Coordination	Perform a forward roll over the gymnastics mats.
5	Coordination	Walk on all fours over an upturned bench.
6	Jumping power	Jump over the box and run with high knees over the crash mat.

 * = critical exercise (constant supervision required)
 ( ) = the number of apparatus assemblies recommended to avoid waiting times

Lesson 2   *Simple Jumps*

Introduction

The second sample lesson introduces all the jumps and vaults commonly performed in parkour. These are required very frequently and are thus an important part of the standard repertoire of moves. As such, it is essential that all pupils learn them. As with the first lesson, the teacher can assume that the majority of pupils will be able to complete all the exercises and target movements. The level of difficulty can be varied by modifying the box heights. Since these jumps are easy to teach and simple to perform, the author has foregone a systematic sequence of introductory exercises, in favour of exercises for developing general strength and jumping power.

1. Warm-up

No.	Activity	P	Materials	Illustration
Running exercise				
1	Run one circuit backwards.	↻ 1	-	
2	With a partner: both partners stand face to face, at arm's length from each other. Both run in this position at a relaxed speed. The partner running forward guides the other using light hand pressure on the shoulder, to avoid him colliding with other participants. When the instructor gives the signal, the partners change over.	✗ 2	-	
3	Both partners stand face to face and run one circuit in sidesteps. While doing so, they jump and clap the other's hands.	↻ 2	-	

Warm-up course: See end of lesson: Warm-up course - Assembly 2

2. 1. Crane jump

Materials: Box comprising five sections, positioned longways, with a landing mat sideways behind it.
Note: Always make the approach jump towards the narrow side of a high box, to avoid knocking it over.

Target movement

1. Take a short approach towards the narrow side of the box, and take off from one leg, with the free leg strongly bent.

2. Land on the box with the ball of the foot of the free leg, stabilising the landing by briefly pressing the tip of the following foot onto the front of the box, while maintaining balance with the arms.

3. Pull the following leg onto the box and continue running.

Materials: Large boxes, small boxes, landing mats.

Exercises

1. Power and stability exercise on low box: stand at the edge of the box on one leg.

2. Lower the free leg ...

3. ... and raise it again. Repeat the movement several times and then change legs.

1. Low jumps from the small box: take a small step forwards with one leg, keeping the standing leg stretched. Swing the arms up, keeping them bent at the elbows.

2. Land on the front of the feet with both legs together. Swing the arms back, still bent at the elbows. Bend the knees slightly and immediately push off again, without the heels touching the ground.

3. At the precise moment of pushing off from the floor, swing the arms forwards and upwards. Land on the box with the legs together.

1. Take off from a small box with one leg.

2. Land on the box with the foot of the free leg. Press the tip of the following foot onto the front of the box to stabilise the landing.

3. Perform a drop onto the landing mat. Bend knees on landing (not less than 90°) using arms for support if necessary (see 7.6). Repeat exercise. Take an approach run and jump onto the small box.

2. 2. Lazy vault – Passement/passe de barrière

Materials: Box, four-sections (or horse of similar height) with a landing mat placed behind, sideways on.

Target movement

1. Take a run-up at a 45° angle to the box. Place the left arm on the left-hand side of the box for support. The last step before the box ends with the right foot diagonally in front of the left foot.

2. Stretch out the left (free) leg in front of the box and swing it high, pushing off from the right leg, using the left arm for support. Slide the hip forward during the jump. Swing the right arm upwards to support the swing motion.

3. Support the flight phase over the box by swinging the arm out backwards. Land behind the box in a step position (here, with the right foot in front of the left foot). This enables the immediate transition to running after landing.

2. 3. Kong vault/monkey vault/cat jump – Saut de chat

Materials: Box, five-sections (or horse of similar height) with a landing mat placed behind, sideways on.

Target movement

1. Push off from the ground with both legs and place hands on the box.

2. Place both hands simultaneously on the box. Tuck legs up tightly beneath the body.

3. Once the legs have passed through, push off strongly with both hands.

When the hands are set down for support twice in succession during a kong vault over a long obstacle (or lengthways box) or two successive obstacles, the move is referred to as a "king kong vault".

2. 4. Speed vault/lateral vault – Passement

Materials: Box, four-sections (or horse of similar height) with two landing mats placed behind, sideways on.

Target movement

1. Take a diagonal or frontal run-up to the box and take off from one leg.
Note: the hands are only placed on the box after take off, during the flight phase.

2. The free leg is bent at the knee in a horizontal position beneath the body. The take-off leg is initially bent horizontally at the knee and then gradually stretched out to the front as the vault progresses. One arm is placed on the box for support (here: left).

3. Land on the box with legs in a step position, with the take-off leg touching down first after a long, ground-covering step.

Materials: Large box, landing mats.

Exercises

1. Take a diagonal run-up to the box and take off from one leg. Place one hand on the top of the box for support (here: left).

2. Bend the free leg at the knee and slide it over the box on the hip side. The take-off leg is stretched out to the side, raised slightly so as not to touch the box.

3. Land on the box with the legs in a step position.

1. Step vault: single-legged take-off. One hand is placed on the top of the box for support (here: left).

2. Land on the box with the outstretched leg (here: right) and swing the other leg (here: left) through the supporting limbs.

3. Land on the box with legs in a step position.

2. **5. Lateral vault – Passement**

Materials: Box, four-sections (or horse of similar height) with two landing mats placed behind, sideways on.

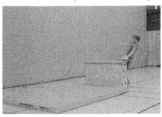   

Target movement

1. Take off from one leg. At the moment of take-off, stretch the left hand forward towards the box.

2. Place the hand on the top edge of the box in the support phase. Swing legs together over the box, keeping them parallel.

3. Land behind the box with the legs together, or move directly into a run.

3. **Suggested games:** Equipment rounders (see Game 4)

4. **Relaxation:** See ch. 9, exercises 2, 6, 17, 22, 27, 38

Warm-up course   Assembly 2

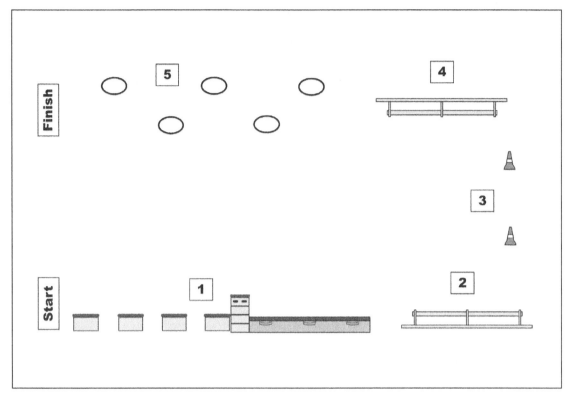

Number	Materials	Number	Materials
5	Hoops	1	Crash mat
4	Small boxes	2	Benches
1	Large box	2	Cones

Stage	Object of exercise	Explanation
Start		Participants pass through the course individually, progressing from start to finish.
1*	Jumping power	Jump from box to box (maximum distance 50cm) and perform a stretch jump from the large box onto the crash mat.
2	Coordination	Walk backwards over a bench (upright or upturned).
3	Coordination and jumping power	Walk backwards over a bench (upright or upturned).
4	Coordination and support power	Perform turn vaults over a bench.
5	Speed	Run zigzag from one hoop to the next, reaching into each hoop and touching the floor with the hand.

* = critical exercise (constant supervision required)

Lesson 3　　　*Reverse Vaults*

Reverse vaults are moves that require great coordination, since they involve an unusual sequence of body movements. However, by taking a gradual and systematic approach, they are quite easy to learn. In the early stages, it is advisable to practice from standing or from a short run-up, and to slowly increase speed (see Exercises).

Introduction

1.　Warm-up

No.	Activity	P	Materials	Illustration

Running exercise

1　Run one circuit alternating between quiet and loud steps, when told to do so by the instructor.　　1　-

2　Run one circuit alternately forwards and backwards, when told to do so by the instructor.　　1　-

3　Run one circuit and when told to do so by the instructor, perform a complete turn about the axis of the body, each time ending with a squat.　　1　-

4　Run one circuit in side steps, crossing the legs alternately in front of and behind the body.　　1　-

Warm-up course: See end of lesson: Warm-up course - Assembly 3

2.　1. Lazy vault reverse

Materials: Box, three-sections (or horse of similar height) with a landing mat placed behind and sideways on. Make two floor markings in front of the box to indicate the running path and push-off points (see fig.).
Note: Decide beforehand which leg to take off from.

1. Here, the movement is shown from the left: take a run-up at an angle of 45° to the box.

2. Touch the right foot on the first marking in front of the box, roughly in the middle in the direction of the run.

3. The left foot reaches the second marking with a 90° turn to the right, one foot-length in front of the box; at the same time, the upper torso turns to the right. Keep looking over the right shoulder.

Target movement

Target movement

4. Coming out of this hip twist, the right arm is placed on the right side of the box behind the back for support, and the right leg swung immediately over the box.

5. Push off from the ground with the left leg while retaining the support of the right arm.

2. Reverse vault (on box or horizontal bar)

Materials: Large box sideways on, four sections, and a landing mat placed behind, sideways.

Target movement

1. Take a run-up at a 45° angle to the box. Stretch out the support arm towards the top of the box. Take off turning backwards with both legs.

2. Place the support arm (here: right) on the box, and perform a backward turn over the box with legs tucked.

3. Land with both legs together or in a step position, moving immediately into a run.

Materials: Benches, landing mats, springboards, large box.

Exercises

1. From standing: take off turning backwards on one leg over a bench or similar low obstacle. Alternatively, jump over a rope marking on the floor.

2. Cross over the bench backwards, looking over the shoulder.

3. Land behind the bench with legs together. Repeat movement from a run-up at a 45° angle to the box with legs held constantly together.

1. Perform a turn vault from standing over the sideways box with the aid of a springboard.

2. Make an intermediate landing on the box with legs together.

3. Take off behind the box with the legs together.

1. Perform a turn vault over the sideways box from standing with the aid of a springboard.

2. Jump over the box without landing first. The body's CofG rests over the support surface of the hands.

3. Land behind the box with legs together.

1. Take off backwards with both legs from a tilted springboard. Place one hand on the top of the box for support (here: right).

2. After turning through 180°, make an intermediate landing on the box with legs closed.

3. Land behind the box using the right arm for support.

Repeat movement from a run-up.

1. Stand at an angle to the box and place one hand on the top of the box (here: right).

2. Take off backwards with both legs and land on top of the box in a squat with both legs together. Keep hand on box for constant support.

3. Land behind the box with legs closed. Repeat the movement: turn body gradually more and more until you are able to land with your back to the box.

Exercises

Materials: A horizontal bar mounted somewhat below hip height, with a springboard to the front and a landing mat behind, set sideways on.

1. The move is performed over the right-hand side of the body. Starting from a standing position on the springboard, hold on to the horizontal bar with a mixed grip to the front left of the body.

2. Push off strongly from the springboard, with both legs together, and turn. Shift the CofG to the supporting arms.

3. While crossing over the horizontal bar, turn the body over the left-shoulder side, beginning with a push-off from the springboard.

4. As soon as the legs pass over the bar, release the left hand from the bar to support the body through an upper torso opening.

5. Release the hands and land with the back to the bar, moving straight into a run.

Repeat the movement: perform the movement from a run-up and without a springboard.

3. **Suggested games:** Equipment catch (see Game 2)

4. **Relaxation:** See ch. 9, exercises 1, 7, 25, 29, 36

| Warm-up course | Assembly 3 |

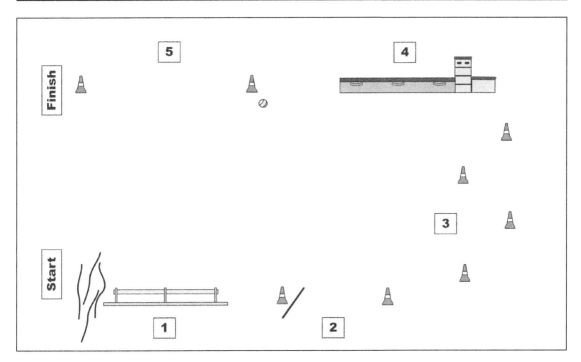

Number	Materials	Number	Materials	Number	Materials
4	Ropes	8	Cones	2	Benches
2	Tennis balls	2	Balance bars	1	Crash mat
1	Large box	1	Small box		

Stage	Object of exercise	Explanation
Start		The course is to be completed in running by two partners, with each partner holding onto the same rope. The course can also be completed by one partner **blindfold**, with the other partner guiding him with a rope, held such that their hands are a short distance away from each other.
1 (2)	Coordination	Both partners balance over the upturned bench, one forwards, the other backwards. **Blindfold course:** One partner balances along the upturned bench.
2 (2)	Coordination	Partners stand next to each other on one leg, holding the balance bar between their raised feet, and then walk through the cones, keeping in balance (3 m). **Blindfold course:** Roll the sideways-lying balance bar over the floor with the sole of the foot.
3 (2)	Coordination	Partners stand back to back and run sideways through the widely spaced cones in a wide slalom, without losing body contact.
4	Coordination and Jumping power	Walk over the box arrangement and perform a stretch jump onto the crash mat. **Blindfold course:** Only one partner walks over the boxes.
5	Coordination	Partners stand opposite each other, each holding onto a rope, such that their hands are a short distance away from each other, passing the tennis ball from one to the other between the cones with their feet. **Blindfold course:** Fast race (without a ball).

( ) = the number of apparatus assemblies recommended to avoid waiting times

Lesson 4   *Dash Vault and Underbar*

Introduction

The defining feature of these jumps is that they are performed with the feet to the front. Although it looks unusual, it can also be rather impressive, because the jumper must ensure that his feet have a clear path over the obstacle. It is virtually impossible to correct any errors once the vault has commenced, the result of which can be an uncontrolled fall, for which reason it is not recommended that the training session begins directly with the target move. In the sample lesson, the move is introduced gradually, to allow pupils to learn to trust in their own abilities. The underbar is similar to the dash vault, except that the hands do not hold on to an object below the body for support, but are extended upwards towards an overhead object. The majority of pupils can be expected to cope with these vaults.

1. Warm-up

No.	Activity	P	Materials	Illustration
Running exercise				
1	Run one circuit to loosen up.	1	-	
2	When instructed to do so, run one circuit with fast, short steps (5 seconds each).	1	-	
3	Run one circuit touching the floor lines of the hall, followed by a whole turn around the body's longitudinal axis.	1	-	

Warm-up course: See end of lesson: Warm-up course - Assembly 4

2.   1. Dash vault – Passement

Materials: Large box, five sections, with two landing mats placed behind, sideways on.

Target movement

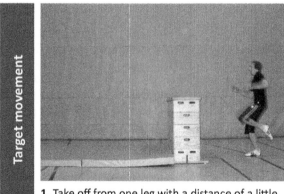 

1. Take off from one leg with a distance of a little more than one leg length.

2. Lift legs up explosively into a horizontal position.

3. Once the legs have passed over the obstacle, push off strongly from the box with both hands.

4. Land behind the box with legs together or in step position. The considerable vaulting distance that can be covered by pushing off with the hands requires two landing mats behind the box for safety.

Materials: Crash mats, large box, landing mats.

Take a short run-up and jump onto a crash mat with legs stretched forward.
The upper torso remains upright and the arms provide lateral support on the crash mat.

Repeat the move with two crash mats one above the other.

Repeat the move, now with three crash mats one above the other.

Repeat the move, placing a four-section box in front of the stack of three crash mats. The box is used as a push-off surface for the hands during the vault.

Remove all the crash mats apart from one. This time land in a standing rather than a sitting position.

Replace the crash mat with two landing mats, positioned sideways.

Exercises

2. 2. Underbar/clearing – Franchissement

Materials: Double bars, one vertically above the other, at shoulder height and at hip height.
Hang a soft gymnastics mat over the lower bar, with two landing mats lying sideways behind the bars.
Note: Two spotters must be in place behind the horizontal bars to prevent the jumper from falling backwards onto the lower bar.

Target movement

1. Run towards the double bars, take off from one foot, and perform a dash vault (with the feet ahead) through the space between the bars.

2. Once the legs have passed between the bars, grip the top bar with an overhand grip. As the angle between the arms and the torso opens and the pulling force on the bar increases, strengthen the forward swing.

3. Land with legs closed or in step position. Move the arms ahead when landing, to avoid falling backwards.

Materials: Horizontal bars, soft gymnastics mat, crash mats, ropes, landing mats.

Exercises

1. With the horizontal bar at chest height, perform a forward swing over the rope marking on the floor, beginning from a standing position. Hold the horizontal bar in an overhand grip and bend the arms slightly.
The tensioned leg is under or slightly in front of the bar. Lunge out with the free leg.

2. Swing the thighs up to the horizontal bar. If the CofG oscillates beneath the bar, perform a fast and powerful hip stretch (underswing movement through the opening of the leg-torso angle). Open the arm-torso angle further to raise the CofG to the level of the bar.
Note: Avoid hollowing the back!

3. Upon landing, bring the arms forward to avoid falling backwards.

Repeat the exercise, but performing the move from a run-up.

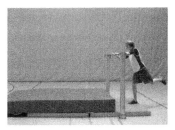

1. Assemble the horizontal bar at chest or shoulder height. Perform an underswing onto a crash mat: hold the horizontal bar in an overhand grip. Tense the arms slightly. Set the tensioned leg beneath or slightly in front of the bar. Begin swing with the free leg.

2. Keep legs closed in forward swing and swing feet far ahead through the opening of the arm-torso angle up to the height of the horizontal bar.

3. Release the hands and land on the crash mat in a sitting position.

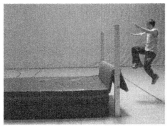

1. Position the horizontal bar at hip height and cover with soft gymnastics mat for protection. Place crash mats, one above the other, longways behind the bar. Take a short run-up and take off from one leg at a distance of about one leg length from the bar.

2. Jump over the lower bar with a dash vault, without pushing off with the hands.

3. Land on the crash mats in a sitting position.

1. Double bars: take a short run-up and take off from one leg at a distance of about one leg length from the bar.

2. First jump through the space between the bars with both legs outstretched, then grip the upper bar with both hands in an overhand grip and pull the body through.

3. Land on the crash mat in a sitting position.

3. **Suggested games:** Shoot-out (see Game 3)

4. **Relaxation:** See ch. 9, exercises 6, 8, 14, 15, 23

Exercises

Warm-up course   **Assembly 4**

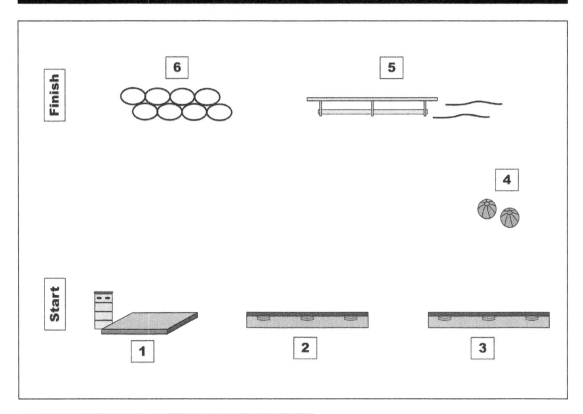

Number	Materials	Number	Materials
1	Large box	1	Bench
1	Landing mat	2	Medicine balls
2	Crash mats	8	Hoops
2	Skipping ropes		

Stage	Object of exercise	Explanation
Start		Participants pass through the course individually, progressing from start to finish.
1	Jumping power	Jump onto the box and jump down onto the landing mat.
2	Arm power	Collapse onto the crash mat along the length of the body and drag yourself by the hands to the end of the mat.
3	Power endurance	Skip on the crash mat.
4 (2)	Arm power	Throw a medicine ball against the wall three times and catch it again. Wall distance approx. 2m.
5 (2)	Coordination	Run over the bench while skipping.
6	Coordination	Step quickly into the hoops with alternating feet.

( ) = the number of apparatus assemblies recommended to avoid waiting times

Lesson 5   *Spiral Underbar*

The spiral underbar is a useful move whenever there is no object nearby to hold on to. The spiral motion allows a powerful and long take-off to be combined with a compact and safe posture. This move requires good jumping power and coordination skill. It is, however, easy to learn, by applying a systematic approach.

Introduction

1. Warm-up

No.	Activity	P	Materials	Illustration
Running exercise				
1	Run sideways on all fours along the floor with wide outwardly reaching steps.	1	-	
2	Run on the floor lines only.	1	-	
3	Crawl on all fours, on the floor lines only.	1	-	
4	Jump from one floor line to the next with legs together.	1	-	
5	Jump from one floor line to the next with legs together, however with a single-leg jump in-between.	1	-	

Warm-up course: See end of lesson: Warm-up course - Assembly 5

2. 1. Spiral underbar

Materials: Asymmetrical bars, landing mats.

1. Perform a turning take-off in front of the lower bar and bring the arms out to the front.

2. In the flight phase, pass by the side of the lower bar and stretch out the arms at head height, bringing the hands into a mixed grip position.

3. Grip the upper bar in a mixed grip and at the same time, swing the legs backwards over the lower bar, slightly bent.

Target movement

Target movement

4. Continue the turn and release one hand from the bar (here: right). Keep the legs closed.

5. Shortly after, release the other hand from the upper bar.

6. Land on the landing mats behind the asymmetrical bars with legs together or in a step position, and continue running.

Materials: Asymmetrical bars, landing mats, rubber cord, cones, gymnastics mat.

Grip instructions for the exercises: grip the upper bar in a mixed grip, crossed. In the target movement, this grip is resolved into a normal mixed grip by virtue of the position of the back with respect to the lower bar when jumping towards the upper bar. See picture 3 on page 65.

Exercises

1. Squat on the lower bar and hold onto the upper bar in a crossed mixed grip.

2. Dismount from the lower bar and turn the body through a half turn to resolve the crossed grip.

3. Come down backwards landing in a step position sideways to the bar and move directly into a run.

1. Perform a spiral underbar on the horizontal bar or asymmetrical bars over a rope marking on the floor: take off from in front of the rope with a turn and move the hands into a mixed grip position.

2. Perform the turn in reverse and release the hands one after the other from the horizontal bar.

3. Come down backwards landing in a step position sideways to the bar and move directly into a run.

1. Stand sideways and reach forwards to grasp the upper bar in a crossed mixed grip.

2. Push off and turn from both legs, at the same time pulling on the upper bar with the arms, initially with the side of the hip on the mat covering the lower bar.

3. Resolve the crossed mixed grip by turning onto the back.

4. Pull the legs over the mat, tightly tucked in.

5. Perform a complete turn (360°) and set down with the feet beneath the higher bar.

Replace the lower bar with a rubber cord and perform the move from a run-up.

3. **Suggested games:** Not necessary due to the great demands of the main activity.

4. **Relaxation:** See ch. 9, exercises 3, 5, 16, 18, 26

Warm-up course | **Assembly 5**

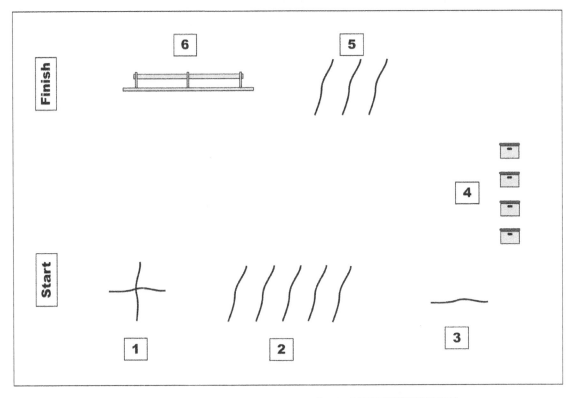

Number	Materials	Number	Materials	Number	Materials
11	Skipping ropes	4	Small boxes	1	Bench

Stage	Object of exercise	Explanation
Start		Participants pass through the course individually, progressing from start to finish.
1	Coordination	Jump clockwise on one leg from square to square. Repeat in the other direction.
2	Coordination	Climb over the ropes backwards on all fours without touching it.
3	Power endurance	Adopt the press-up position, with both hands touching the floor on the side of the rope. From this position, jump five times with both hands over the rope, each time landing back in the press-up position.
4	Jumping power	Jump from the floor onto the box from the right leg, take off from the box from both legs, then jump onto the next box from the left leg, etc.
5	Coordination	Jump over each rope with the legs together. Perform half a turn around the body's axis with each jump. Repeat the exercise with whole turns.
6	Coordination	Walk on all fours over an upturned bench.

( ) = the number of apparatus assemblies recommended to avoid waiting times

Lesson 6   *The Roll*

Introduction

The roll in parkour is similar to the judo roll and its purpose is to dispel the energy from long or drop jumps. Unlike the judo roll, it is performed from a slight step position, as commonly encountered after a drop. In the following examples, both hands touch the ground, since beginners generally consider this easier to do and do it intuitively (more advanced pupils commonly land directly on their shoulder and perform the roll from this position).

Although rolling over the floor is safe to practice, caution should be taken when extending the jumping distance, to avoid compression injuries from deficiently performed jumps.

1. Warm-up

No.	Activity	P	Materials	Illustration
Running exercise				
1	Run two circuits: light jogging in the curves and with low knees in the straights. **Note:** *Maintain a knee angle of over 90° to protect the joints!*	↻ 1	-	
2	Run one circuit with heels swinging up to the buttocks. **Note:** *Step quietly.*	↻ 1	-	
3	Run one circuit and, when instructed to do so, do a complete turn about the body's axis, followed by a short sprint. **Note:** *Step quietly.*	↻ 1	-	

Warm-up course: See end of lesson: Warm-up course - Assembly 6

2. 1. Basic roll (following a drop jump) – Roulade (saut de fond)

Materials: Landing mats, table or other raised plateau.

Target movement

1. Jump from the table with both legs. Keep feet together and parallel with knees slightly bent.

2. Land on the front feet with knees bent somewhat more than 90°. Don't let the heels touch the floor! Shift your body weight immediately forward and move one shoulder forward (here: left). Then lower the upper torso and lay the back of the front arm along with the other hand on the floor (with the fingers pointing towards each other).

Target movement

3. Allow the body to roll in an arc over the left shoulder and arm. Lay the head to the side and tuck the chin into the chest.

4. Allow the swing to bring the body back into the standing position and continue running.

Materials: Landing mats, large box, gymnastics mats, medicine balls.

Exercises

1. Jump off the box from both legs. Keep your eyes fixed on the landing position.

2. Land gently on the balls of your feet with knees bent somewhat more than 90° and torso leaning forward.

3. Set the hands down and crawl on in this position. Keep watching ahead.

4. Gradually straighten the upper torso and run now only on the balls of your feet.

1. Roll on the floor: maintain a shoulder wide step position, with hands and arms forming a circle in front of the body, and fingers pointing towards each other.

2. Shift the body weight to the front foot and lower the upper torso to allow the hands to set down on the floor. Tuck the chin into the chest and lay the head to one side.

3. Move the shoulder and arm forward and perform the roll over them. Roll diagonally over the back (here from the left shoulder to the right hip).

4. Use the force of the swing to bring the body back into the standing position and continue running.

1. Jump off the large box and go into a roll.

2. First land on the feet in a slight step position with a knee angle of somewhat more than 90°. Do not set the heels down! Repeat the exercise with the feet setting down increasingly parallel to each other.

3. Set down the back of the lower arm and the palm of the other hand. When rolling, tuck the chin into the chest and lay the head to one side.

4. Allow the swing to bring the body back into the standing position and continue running.

1. Roll over a distance (using a gymnastics mat): Take off from one leg from a floor marking.

2. Perform a dive over a gymnastics mat with arms stretched out forward.

3. Set the back of the lower arm (here: left) and the palm of the other hand (here: right) down on the floor and continue the roll over the shoulder and arm (here: left) and diagonally over the back. Tuck the chin into the chest and lay the head to one side.

4. Use the force of the swing to bring the body back into the standing position and continue running.

1. Roll over a low obstacle (e.g. medicine balls): take off from one leg from a floor marking.

2. Perform a dive over the medicine balls. Set the back of the lower arm (here: left) and the palm of the other hand (here: right) down on the floor. Lay the head to one side (here: right).

3. Continue the roll over the shoulder and arm (here: left) and diagonally over the back. Tuck the chin into the chest and lay the head to one side. Keep the upper torso rounded during the roll.

4. Use the force of the swing to bring the body back into the standing position and continue running.

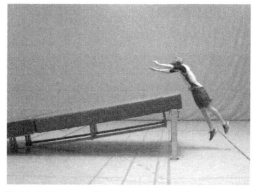

1. Take off from a run-up onto an inclined crash mat, placed with one end on a horizontal bar and supported by two benches.

2. Maintain a stretched posture with arms stretched out to the front.

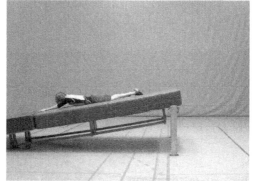

3. Jump far ahead onto the crash mat.
Note: Do not use the hands for support.

4. Land on the front of the body, in an outstretched position.

1. Run up towards the inclined crash mat and take off from one leg.

2. Perform a dive as high – and landing as far along the crash mat – as possible.

3. After setting down the hands, roll over the shoulder and arm.

4. Come out of the roll kneeling on one leg.

1. For advanced students:
Roll out of a dive from a high obstacle: take off from one leg in front of the obstacle.

2. Dive over a box covered for protection. Set the back of the lower arm (here: left) and the palm of the other hand (here: right) down on the floor. Immediately upon setting down, allow the arms to yield and tuck the chin into the chest.

3. Continue the roll over the shoulder and arm (here: left) and diagonally over the back. Tuck the chin into the chest and lay the head to one side.

4. Allow the swing to bring the body back into the standing position.

3. **Suggested games:** Not necessary due to the great demands of the main activity.

4. **Relaxation:** See ch. 9, exercises

Warm-up course   Assembly 6

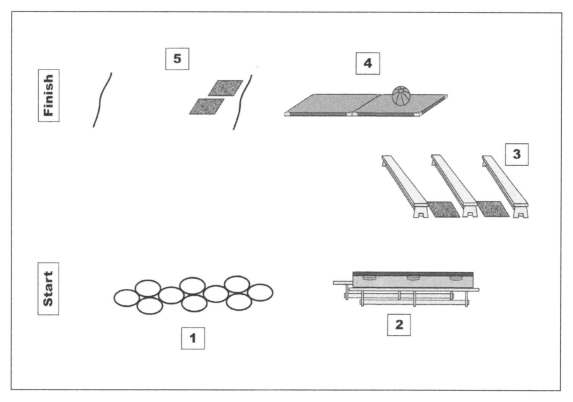

Number	Materials	Number	Materials	Number	Materials
2	Skipping ropes	5	Benches	2	Gymnastics mats
10	Hoops	4	Carpet tiles	1	Medicine ball
1	Crash mats				

Stage	Object of exercise	Explanation
Start		Participants pass through the course individually, progressing from start to finish.
1	Coordination and speed	Jump with closed legs from one hoop into two hoops and back into one.
2*	Mentally overcoming an obstacle	Crawl beneath a crash mat which lies atop two benches.
3 (2)	Power endurance	Sit on a carpet tile and drag yourself between and past the benches using only your arms.
4	Coordination	Perform a forward roll (or dive roll) over a medicine ball.
5	Power endurance	Stand on one leg on a carpet tile and push yourself along the floor with the other leg (as if your were riding a scooter).

* = critical exercise (constant supervision required)

( ) = the number of apparatus assemblies recommended to avoid waiting times

Lesson 7   *Wall Run*

Introduction

The wall run can be used to overcome surprisingly high and long obstacles. As a rule, there should be no contact with the obstacle itself during the run. A wall run (or tic tac) comprises two or more steps taken against a wall. However, it is advisable to begin learning the move with one step; this is sufficient for overcoming obstacles up to around chest height. Increasing the number of steps over the wall also enables the runner to overcome a longer distance.

The wall run is also often used to access high obstacles (see Wall up).

1. Warm-up

No.	Activity	P	Materials	Illustration
Running exercise				
1	Put half tennis balls down along the oval at irregular intervals: run one circuit, running around each ball once.	1	Half tennis ball	
2	As with 1, but keeping the shoulder axis pointing in the running direction as you circle each tennis ball.	1	Half tennis ball	
3	As with 1, but tapping the tennis balls with one foot. **Note:** *Bend the knees.*	1	Half tennis ball	
4	As with 1, but tapping the tennis balls alternately with the left and right hands.	1	Half tennis ball	

Warm-up course: See end of lesson: Warm-up course - Assembly 7

2. 1. Wall run – Tic-tac

Materials: Landing mats, crash mat, wall.

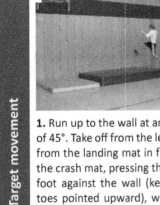

Target movement

1. Run up to the wall at an angle of 45°. Take off from the left foot from the landing mat in front of the crash mat, pressing the right foot against the wall (keep the toes pointed upward), with the knee clearly bent.

2. Perform a second step against the wall with the left foot (toes pointing upward!); while pushing off, turn the upper torso and head towards the landing position.
Note: when making two or three steps against the wall, push off from each step making each step taken higher than the previous one. This will result in you running diagonally up the wall in short, fast steps.

3. After pushing off with the foot against the wall, land on the landing mat behind the crash mat and continue running.

Materials: Landing mats, large box, small box, gymnastics mat.

Take off from one leg from the front gymnastics mat towards the wall. Land on the rear landing mats.

Jumping over an obstacle: take off from the floor with the left leg. Push off from the wall above the box with the right leg. Land on the landing mats behind the box.

See the previous move: Raise the obstacle and use a take-off aid.

See the previous move: Raise the obstacle and jump without a take-off aid.
Variation: position the obstacle in a corner and perform the push off from two sides of the wall.

By placing the arm furthest from the wall onto the box for support, you can increase your safety when passing over the obstacle or even "rescue" an unsuccessful jump.

Jump over a sideways-standing obstacle after pushing off from the wall, using a take-off aid. Land on the landing mat.

1. Run up at a 45° angle to the wall. Take off from one leg from the landing mat (here: left leg).

2. Press the right leg against the wall behind the sideways-standing box, and jump over the box.

3. Land behind the box on the landing mat, bending at the knees

3. **Suggested games:** Timing (see Game 5)

4. **Relaxation:** See ch. 9, exercises

Exercises

Warm-up course	Assembly 7

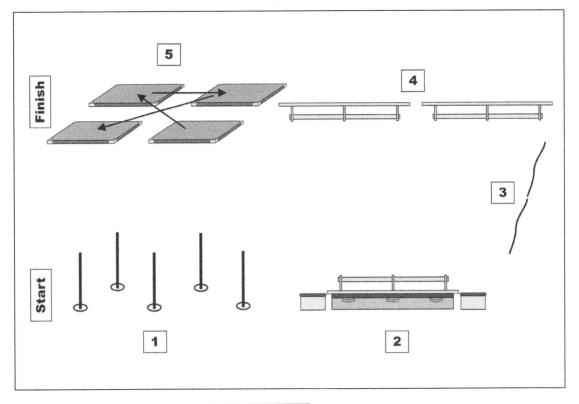

Number	Materials	Number	Materials
4	Gymnastics mats	3	Benches
5	Poles and stands	2	Skipping ropes
2	Small boxes	1	Crash mat

Stage	Object of exercise	Explanation
Start		Participants pass through the course individually, progressing from start to finish.
1	Speed	Run around the poles in a slalom.
2	Coordination	Balance along an upturned bench placed on a crash mat. **Note:** *Use boxes for help at start and finish!*
3	Jumping power	Hop on one leg over the ropes in a zigzag.
4	Support power	In a press-up position: Place hands on floor for support and the tips of the feet on the bench. Move arms and legs slowly sideways without abandoning the press-up position.
5	Stamina and speed	Lie face down on the first mat, get up quickly and sprint to the mat diagonally opposite, and lie down again face down. Get up again quickly and run backwards to the mat behind, again lying face down afterwards. Get up quickly and run diagonally to the final mat, and lie down again.

Lesson 8   *Cat Leap and Wall Up*

Introduction

The cat leap or arm jump is a move used for jumping towards objects on which it is not possible to land directly. The object must display some kind of edge or other feature that can be gripped with the hands. The feet are pulled in beneath the body and the balls of the feet are pressed against the obstacle for support. The feet are also important when subsequently pushing off from the obstacle. While the arm jump and wall up originate from parkour, the modified wall up in the target movement stems from freerunning, as does the complete body turn.

1. Warm-up

No.	Activity	P	Materials	Illustration
Running exercise				
1	Perform a number of simple jumping exercises while running a circuit: Make several consecutive closed-leg jumps along the straight sections of the oval. **Note:** *Step quietly.*	1	-	
2	As with 1 above, but hopping on one leg. **Note:** *Step quietly.*	1	-	
3	As with 1 above, but hopping sideways **Note:** *Insides of feet touch slightly.*	1	-	
4	As with 1 above, but squatting right down, with the hands touching the floor and performing an explosive stretch jump. **Note:** *Repeat exercise several times.*	1	-	

Warm-up course: See end of lesson: Warm-up course - Assembly 8

2. 1. Arm jump/cat leap – Saut de bras

Materials: Box, five sections, placed longways, with one landing mat behind it sideways on, also an upturned crash mat or gymnastics mat turned sideways and leant against a section of wall bars, secured with ropes.

1. Perform a closed-legged jump from standing from a longways-standing box onto the wall bars.

2. Hold onto the wall bars with outstretched arms and, adopting a squat position, press the front feet against the upturned crash mat.

Target movement

Variations and combinations

Materials: Large box, four/five sections, placed longways, with one landing mat behind it sideways on. Also an upturned crash mat or gymnastics mat turned sideways and leant against a section of wall bars, secured with ropes.

Exercises

1. Take a run-up and run first over a small and then a large box.

2. Jump in a tucked position against the crash mat and at the same time grip the wall bars.

1. Jump in a tucked position against the crash mat and at the same time grip the wall bars.

2. Perform a powerful, turning push-off backwards towards the second set of wall bars, onto which a mat has been secured.

3. Jump in a squat position against the wall bars or mat, while at the same time gripping the wall bars.

2. 360° wall up

Materials: A sideways upturned crash mat (firm) leant against a section of wall bars, secured with ropes, also landing mats.

Target movement

1. Take a run-up at an angle of 45° to the wall. Push off from the floor towards the crash mat with a turn of approx. 90° (here: left foot).

2. Kick back against the crash mat with the underside of the right foot, to give extra support to the turn. Allow the leg kicking against the crash mat to yield.

3. After pushing off from the crash mat with the right foot, grip the wall bars while tucking up the knees, with the balls of the feet pressing against the crash mat.

Materials: Landing mats, crash mats, ropes for securing.

1. Take a run-up at an angle of 45° to the crash mat. Take off from the floor with one leg and kick against the crash mat with the underside of the foot facing the crash mat, at approximately hip height. Bend the leg pushing against the crash mat considerably, to enable a powerful push-off.

2. Push off from the crash mat and land facing away from the crash mat with feet parallel and a distance between them of roughly hip width.

1. As above: after pushing off from the crash mat with one leg, perform a three-quarter turn with the arms supporting the swing.

2. Land facing the crash mat with feet parallel and a roughly hip-wide distance between them.

3. **Suggested games:** Shoot-out (see Game 3)

4. **Relaxation:** See ch. 9, exercises

Warm-up course **Assembly 8**

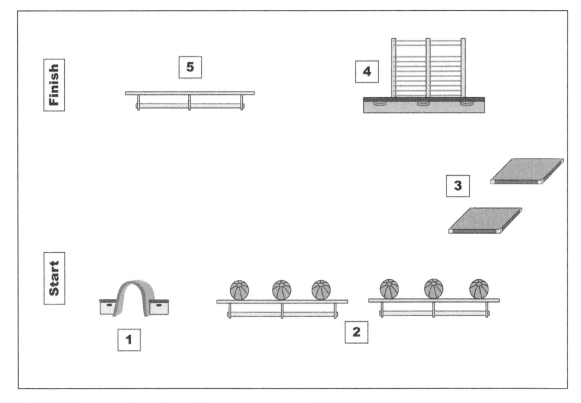

Number	Materials	Number	Materials
2	Small boxes	1	Crash mats
6	Medicine balls	3	Gymnastics mats
3	Benches	1	Wall bars

Stage	Object of exercise	Explanation
Start		Participants pass through the course individually, progressing from start to finish.
1	Coordination	Crawl through a tunnel of mats.
2	Coordination	Balance along the benches without touching the medicine balls.
3	Coordination	Perform a forward roll over each mat.
4	Coordination	Set wall bars at 90° to the wall: climb up the free side of the bars, climb through the upper space, and jump onto the crash mat.
5	Jumping power	Stand on the bench and jump down with the bench between the legs. Jump back onto the bench from this position, etc.

Lesson 9   *Combining Movements*

One of the central aims of parkour is to develop the ability to combine individual moves into a fluid whole (for example within an equipment course or when moving from one apparatus to the next). It is advisable to practice combining transition movements before attempting to apply them in a complex obstacle course. This will serve to emphasise the importance of clean movements and underline the reasoning behind the combinations. This will minimise the risk of losing the flow by attempting to take an un-planned, unsystematic approach to an obstacle. The aim of this lesson is to impart the importance of overcoming obstacles fluidly, systematically, and with control.

Introduction

1.   Warm-up

No.	Activity	P	Materials	Illustration
	Running exercise			
1	When the trainer gives the signal, stop running, fall or go down into a press-up position. From this position, step towards your hands, then stand back up and continue running.	1	-	
2	When instructed to do so by the trainer, stop running, drop onto all fours and crawl in this position in a backwards direction until you reach the wall. Continue the walking motion up the wall until you have attained a handstand position, then return to a normal run.	1	-	
3	When instructed to do so by the trainer, stop running and perform five standing long jumps with your arms on your back, then return to a normal run.	1	-	

Warm-up course: See end of lesson: Warm-up course - Assembly 9

2.   1. Balance to roll

Materials: Small boxes, large boxes, parallel bars, landing mats.

Exercises

1. Balance along parallel bars that have been set up in combination with boxes of increasing height.

2. Continue in this way to the middle of the bars, then turn round to face one bar.

3. Jump down from the bars landing on the landing mat in a step position with both feet reaching the ground at the same time.

4. Shift the weight to the front of the foot and bend down to set your hands on the floor. Place the back of one lower arm and the palm of the other hand on the floor.

5. Perform the roll, using the force of the swing to come into a standing position, then continue running.

2. **2. Kong to roll**

Materials: Large box, landing mats.

1. Push off from the floor with both legs and then place your hands on the box. Place hands on box at the same time. Tuck your legs beneath your body.

2. Push off strongly with both hands, landing first on your feet in a slight step position. Maintain a knee angle of somewhat more than 90° and do not touch the ground with your heels.

3. Set the back of one lower arm and the palm of the other hand on the floor. Pull the chin towards the chest during the roll. Perform the roll, using the force of the swing to come into a standing position, then continue running.

2. **3. Kong to Precision**

Materials: Large box, landing mats, gymnastics mat, soft box.

1. Push off from the floor with both legs and then place the hands on the box.

2. Place both hands on the box at the same time. Tuck your legs beneath your body.

3. Land on the soft box with legs closed and knees bent strongly. Hold arms out in front of your body to stabilise yourself.

2. ### 4. Gap jump to roll

Materials: Large boxes, small boxes, crash mat, gymnastics mat, landing mats.

1. Take a short run-up on the large box, and take off, pushing off with one leg.

2. Place your hands on the crash mat and perform the roll diagonally over one shoulder and along the back.

3. Come out of the roll standing on your knees.

2. ### 5. Tic tac to cat leap

Materials: Landing mat, gymnastics mat, ropes, wall bars.

1. Take a short run-up to the wall, at an angle of 45°.

2. Push off from the floor with one leg and kick against the wall with the other leg at about hip height.

3. Push off backwards from the wall, with the leg strongly bent.

4. Hold on to the wall bars in an overhand grip and pull up the legs beneath the body (cat leap).

Variation: The leg push-off can be assisted by additionally placing the hand on the wall to support and control the rotation.

3. **Suggested games:** Running by numbers (see Game 8)

4. **Relaxation:** See ch. 9, exercises

Warm-up course Assembly 9

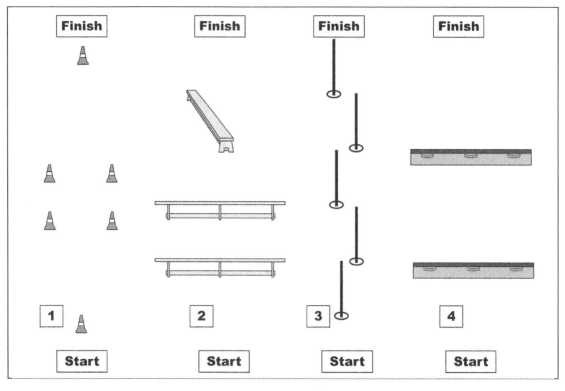

Number	Materials	Number	Materials
6	Cones	5	Poles and stands
2	Crash mats	3	Benches

Stage	Object of exercise	Explanation
Start		The course is completed stage for stage. Pupils begin individually in groups of the same size. After completing three run throughs at one stage, each pupil moves on to the next stage.
1	Coordination and sprinting power	Run into the cone square. There, turn once about the body's axis and sprint immediately to the finish cone.
2	Coordination	Jump over the first sideways bench and crawl through the second one. Perform a side vault over the first section of the longways bench and crawl under the second section of the bench.
3	Coordination and speed	Run backwards in a slalom through the widely spaced stands.
4	Jumping power	Jump with the left leg over the first longways crash mat, and then with the right leg over the second sideways crash mat.

Lesson 10   *Wall Spin*

Introduction

The wall spin is a move that possesses an artistic element and as such originates from the freerunning discipline. Although it is of no use for overcoming obstacles, the unusual movement, comprising a turn about the saggital axis, frequently has motivational value. The move is demanding in terms of coordination but by applying sufficiently systematic exercises, it is quite easy to learn. Many pupils will be able to perform the move all the way up to the inclined crash mat stage (see Exercises), which can be regarded as the final stage of the exercise.

It is up to the participants themselves to recognise which exercises are of use to them and which they would prefer to leave out. The full range of exercises should therefore be offered, to provide a choice.

1. Warm-up

No.	Activity	P	Materials	Illustration
Running exercise				
1	Run one circuit to loosen up.	1	-	
2	Run one circuit backwards with arms raised.	1	-	
3	Run one circuit and hold each elbow forward in turn and attempt to touch it with the diagonally opposed knee. **Note:** *Tap the elbow lightly.*	1	-	

Warm-up course: See end of lesson: Warm-up course - Assembly 10

2. 1. Wall spin

Materials: Landing mats placed in front of a wall.

1. Take a run-up at a 45° angle to the wall. Take off with both legs and hold onto the wall at chest height with both hands, fingers pointing towards the floor. The hands should hold onto the wall, one above the other.

2. With the hands still in position, walk around them with legs squatted.

3. The left arm (supporting arm) remains pressed against the wall until landing sideways on, with legs parallel and open to approximately hip distance.

Target movement

Materials: Benches, medicine balls, springboard, landing mats, small box, crash mat, large boxes.

Exercises

Perform a turn vault over a bench. The CofG is over the supporting arms.

Perform a turn vault over a medicine ball, placed on the bench.

Perform a turn vault over two medicine balls, placed on the bench.

Simple hand grip, with both thumbs pointing towards each other.

Grip with the arm nearest the body turned somewhat inwards, and the fingers of this hand pointing towards yourself. A preliminary tension is created by twisting the arm, which is resolved by the palm spin.

Stand sideways and perform a palm forwards from the springboard after the spring action.
Tip: It is not necessary to perform the full palm spin straightaway. It is also possible to make an interim landing on a parallel bench. With each vault, the angle can be increased.

1. Perform a palm spin on the small box. The torso rests on the supporting arms placed on one edge of the box. The legs are closed.

2. Perform a high palm spin from an arm-support position over the box with a two-legged take-off (swinging body upwards and backwards, pulling the feet towards the buttocks).

3. Once the turn is complete, release the hand from the box and land behind the box in a parallel standing position, sideways on.

1. Perform a palm spin from a parallel standing position. The torso rests over the supporting arms. Take off from two legs.

2. The support phase follows a strong eccentric turning push-off. Guide the body's CofG over the supporting arm (here: left).

3. Land on both legs in parallel, standing sideways on with supporting arm (left) pressing away.

1. Raise two benches at one end in parallel, supported by wall bars. Perform a palm spin over the benches.

2. Make an interim landing on the benches, bend both legs and keep them closed.

3. Jump from the bench into the landing position, standing with legs parallel, sideways to the obstacle.

1. Raise two benches at one end in parallel, supported by wall bars. Perform a palm spin over the benches.

2. Perform a turn over the benches.

3. Land in a parallel standing position, sideways on.
Keep the left hand touching the bench. Repeat the exercise, increasing the inclination of the benches each time.

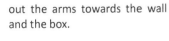  

1. Take a run-up at a 45° angle. Take off from both legs. Stretch out the arms towards the wall and the box.

2. Place one arm on the box for support (here: left). Place the other arm against the wall for support.

3. Land on the landing mat with both legs parallel, sideways on.

Exercises

1. Place a vertically upright landing mat on a small box. The edge of the box must protrude far enough beneath the mat to allow pupils to grip the box with their hands.

2. Jump from standing with both legs.
Note: The angle of the landing mat on the box can be varied according to the pupils' abilities.

3. Land behind the box with legs together in a parallel leg position, sideways on.
Note: Some pupils find this exercise more difficult than the following one.

1. Lean a crash mat at an angle against the wall, using a box for support, with two landing mats to the front. Take a run-up at a 45° angle to the crash mat. Take off from both legs, and place both hands on the crash mat at chest height, with the fingers pointing towards the floor.

2. Bend the legs and rotate body over the supporting arms.

3. After half a turn, take one hand from the mat (here: right).
Note: The feet should guide the turn, with the hip and shoulders following. Do not initiate the turn by moving the shoulder or hip to the front, or the body will collapse after half the distance.

1. Perform a forward wall spin on a standing crash mat.

2. The crash mat provides additional grip because it allows the hands to sink into the foam.

3. Land sideways to the crash mat with legs parallel and open at hip distance.

3. **Suggested games:** Not necessary due to the great demands of the main activity.

4. **Relaxation:** See ch. 9, exercises

Warm-up course   Assembly 10

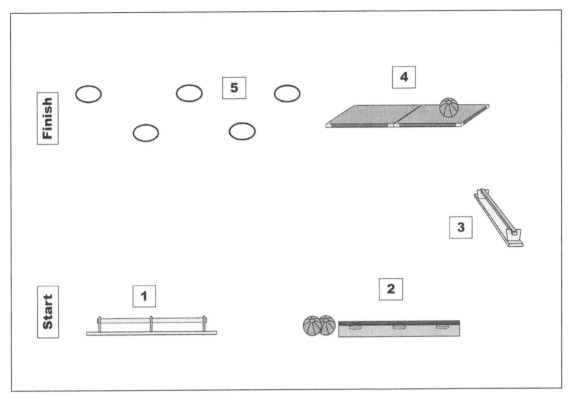

Number	Materials	Number	Materials
2	Benches	1	Crash mat
3	Medicine balls	2	Gymnastics mats
5	Hoops		

Stage	Object of exercise	Explanation
Start		Participants pass through the course individually, progressing from start to finish.
1	Coordination	Balance backwards along the upturned bench.
2	Power endurance	Skip over the crash mat and hold a medicine ball forwards in outstretched arms.
3	Coordination	Balance along an upturned bench and perform two step vaults.
4	Coordination	Perform a roll over a medicine ball without touching it.
5	Jumping power	Jump in a zigzag from hoop to hoop with legs closed (hoops approx. 1.2m apart).

Lesson 11   Wall Flip

Introduction

The wall flip is another artistic movement taken from freerunning. Again, it is a move that is of little use for overcoming obstacles, but it demands great coordination and it is important to ensure constant safety provision while performing the exercises. If there is any interruption to the rotation, there is a great risk of the pupil landing on his head, which can cause compression injuries to the spine. The danger can be minimised by employing a gradual and systematic approach to the exercises to allow pupils to overcome their resistance to the backward turn. In any case, trained spotters must always be directly at hand whenever pupils attempt this move.

1. Warm-up

No.	Activity	P	Materials	Illustration
Running exercise				
1	Run three circuits to loosen up.	1	-	
2	Run with knees raised to the front (high knees). **Note:** *Raise thighs until horizontal!*	1	-	
3	Slow running, interspersed with short bursts of sprinting (for approx. 5m) when told to do so by the instructor.	1	-	

Warm-up course: See end of lesson: Warm-up course - Assembly 11

2. 1. Wallflip

Materials: Landing mats placed in front of a wall.

Target movement

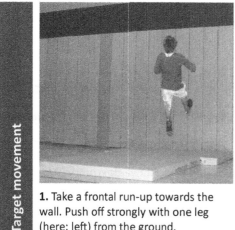

1. Take a frontal run-up towards the wall. Push off strongly with one leg (here: left) from the ground.

2. Run up the wall until the supporting leg (here: right) is pushing horizontally into the wall (above head height). Bend this leg. Bend head back into the nape of the neck (head control is important). **Note:** Depending on the jumping power employed, it may be possible to reach the horizontal position directly from take-off. Otherwise it will be necessary to take one or two steps up the wall to reach the position.

3. Swing the free leg (here: left) through strongly and at constant speed.

4. Land with legs apart at hip distance, facing the wall.

Materials: Horizontal bar, springboard, large boxes, landing mats, crash mats, wedge mat, parallel bars.

1. Swing up using shoulder-high horizontal bar, with the aid of a springboard: grip the bar in a standing position using the overhand grip. Run up to horizontal position with the push-off leg on the springboard. Swing the free leg uniformly alongside the springboard forwards and upwards.

2. Push off strongly from the springboard with the push-off leg and move the hip towards the bar.

3. Rotate into an arm-support position and briefly maintain this position.

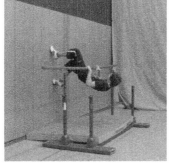

1. Swing up on the bar positioned at chest height in front of a wall: hold bar in overhand grip.

2. Walk two steps up the wall until above the height of the bar, pulling in the arms.

3. Move hip to bar and rotate into an arm-support position.

1. On two crash mats: take a short run-up towards a vertically upright crash mat or wedge mat.

2. Jump onto the crash mat with one leg, slightly bent, at hip height.
Then push off backwards.

3. Land in a standing position, facing the wall.

1. On two crash mats: take a short run-up towards a vertically upright crash mat or wedge mat.

2. Run up the crash mat until both legs are horizontal, with the push-off leg slightly bent.

3. After pushing off from the mat, land on the back (high-jump landing).
Note: Keep the arms to the sides of the body and don't use them for support!
Tuck the chin into the chest.

1. Take a run-up to the tilted crash mat and run up the mat.

2. Perform a backward roll, tucking knees and chin in towards the chest.

3. Land on the feet on the horizontal crash mat.

1. Two spotters clasp the upper arms in a reverse arm grip. Press one leg horizontally against the wedge mat, slightly bent.

2. Perform a wall flip at chest height by swinging the standing leg and at the same time pushing off strongly from the wedge mat.

3. Important: the spotters accompany the pupil until he attains the final standing position.

1. Take a short run-up to the wedge mat. The spotters should stand ready immediately in front of the wedge mat (gesticulating to the pupil to perform the move [GERLING 2002]); arms in front of the body and backs of the hands facing down.

2. The moment the pupil is in the horizontal position (legs and hip above head height when pushing off from the wedge mat), the spotters place one hand on the lower back, above the buttocks and the other hand on the back of the thigh, to help in turning. The knees should be tucked in towards the chest when pushing off from the mat, to lead into a backward roll.

3. **Suggested games:** Not necessary due to the great demands of the main activity.

4. **Relaxation:** See ch. 9, exercises

Warm-up course **Assembly 11**

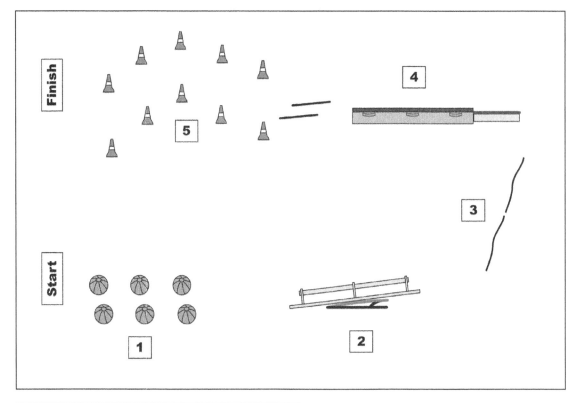

Number	Materials	Number	Materials
6	Medicine balls	1	Crash mats
1	Bench	1	Top box section
1	Springboard	2	Skipping ropes
2	Balance bars	10	Cones

Stage	Object of exercise	Explanation
Start		The course is run through from start to finish. Two participants start as a team.
1 (2)	Coordination	Run over a line of medicine balls without touching the ground.
2*	Coordination	Balance along the wobbly bench, one behind the other.
3	Jumping power	Perform zig-zagging closed-legged jumps, one behind the other, over cords stretched out longways.
4	Jumping power	Jump from the box section as far as you can with your legs closed, onto the crash mat.
5	Coordination	Two partners hold a balance bar at either end. Using the balance bar, one partner helps the other to run backwards through the cone lane. Change positions and repeat.

* = critical exercise (constant supervision required)
( ) = the number of apparatus assemblies recommended to avoid waiting times

Lesson 12   *Wall Up and Turn Vault*

Introduction

Depending on the height of the obstacle, a wall up can consist of a vertical wall run combined with an arm jump. It is an indispensable move in parkour and is used in overcoming high structures, typically walls. When performed athletically, it can be used to overcome obstacles several metres high.
The turn vault is often used to surmount railings in preparation for a drop.

1. Warm-up

No.	Activity		P	Materials	Illustration

Running exercise

1. Walk quickly and clap the hands alternately in front of and behind the body. — 1 — -

2. Run slowly until told to stop by the instructor, then sit down without using the hands and stand up again without using the hands. Repeat the exercise several times. — 1 — -

3. Bend forward and jump on one leg from left to right. The jumps should go as far sideways as possible. Apply plenty of leg swing and arm work when jumping. — 1 — -

Warm-up course: See end of lesson: Warm-up course - Assembly 12

2. 1. Wall up – Passe muraille

Materials: Crash mat, asymmetrical bars, landing mats, large box.

1. Place a crash mat or landing mat in a horizontal orientation between two asymmetrical bars, with the lower bar to the front. Take off from one leg and jump up towards the top of the mat.

2. After halting briefly on the top of the crash mat, jump over it using a turn vault, for example.

3. Land behind the crash mat with your legs apart at hip distance and knees gently bent.
Variation 1: Clamp the crash mat vertically longways between the asymmetrical bars.
Variation 2: Jump from a box onto and over the crash mat (cat leap).
Option: Perform a roll on landing.

Target movement

2. 2. Turn vault – Demi-tour

Materials: Horizontal bars, landing mats.

Target movement

1. Double bars, lower bar at knee height and upper bar at chest height. Hold upper bar in a mixed grip. Stand with the balls of the feet on the lower bar, keeping the feet together. The feet should be oriented vertically beneath the hands.

2. Push off using the spring effect of the lower bar. During the turn vault, one hand moves into an overhand grip (here: right), and the legs and feet remain closed. The supporting arms are employed as much as possible in shifting the CofG. Hold the torso over the bar for as long as possible.

3. Both hands hold onto the bar in an overhand grip.
Tense the legs strongly to perform a landing which is as controlled and gentle as possible, ending on the balls of the feet. The feet should be vertically below the hands as they grip the bar.
Variation: Begin by jumping onto the bar from a small box.

Materials: Horizontal bars, small boxes, landing mats, asymmetrical bars.

Exercises

1. Hold on to the bar at hip height using a mixed grip.

2. Keep the legs and feet closed the whole time.
The supporting arms are employed as much as possible in shifting the CofG.

3. Land sideways to the bar with legs closed (later facing the bar). Keep holding on to the bar with the hand nearest to it during the landing.

1. Raise the bar. Use small boxes to practice landing more precisely.

2. Keep the legs and feet closed the whole time. The supporting arms are employed as much as possible in shifting the CofG.

3. Land sideways on to the bar. Repeat the exercise, turning gradually further until facing the bar.

1. Attach double bars with the lower bar directly over the gymnastics mats and the upper bar at hip height. Hold the bar with the hands in a mixed grip.

2. Keep the legs and feet closed during the jump.
The supporting arms are employed as much as possible in shifting the CofG. One hand changes round (here: right).

3. The two hands are in an overhand grip. The feet are positioned vertically below the hands as they grip.

1. Surmounting a set of asymmetrical bars.
The upper bar should be at hip height above the lower bar. Jump onto the lower bar from a small box with the legs closed.

2. Hold the upper bar in a mixed grip. Stand on the lower bar, keeping the feet closed. Viewed from above, the feet are alongside the hands.

3. . Perform a two-legged take-off using the spring effect of the lower bar. Keep the legs closed. Keep the face constantly turned towards the upper bar. The hands move into an overhand grip.

4. Land on the lower bar with both feet closed, and knees strongly bent.

5. Stretch the legs back from the knees.

6. Release both feet from the lower bar. Dismount over the lower bar using the forward swing and land in a standing position.

3. **Suggested games:** Throw-off (see Game 1)

4. **Relaxation:** See ch. 9, exercises

Exercises

Warm-up course — Assembly 12

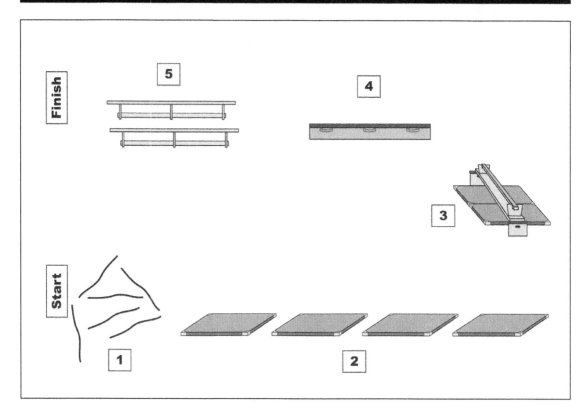

Number	Materials	Number	Materials
6	Skipping ropes	1	Crash mats
6	Landing mats	2	Small boxes
3	Benches		

Stage	Object of exercise	Explanation
Start		Participants pass through the course individually, progressing from start to finish.
1 (6)	Power endurance	Skip with a rope on the spot ten times.
2	Jumping power	Hop over the mats on one leg without touching the spaces in between (approx. 50 cm). Repeat sequence using the other leg.
3*	Coordination	Balance on the raised, upturned bench.
4	Jumping power	Perform three stretch jumps from a low squat on a crash mat.
5 (2)	Support power and jumping power	Perform turn vaults over a bench.

* = critical exercise (constant supervision required)

( ) = the number of apparatus assemblies recommended to avoid waiting times

Lesson 13   *Climbing, Muscling Up and Jumping*

Introduction

Climbing is employed when it is not possible to surmount an obstacle by jumping. Such situations are commonly encountered outdoors, which is why climbing is one of the fundamental disciplines of parkour. It takes a certain effort to recreate such obstacles in a sports hall, but the unusual nature of the apparatus itself is usually enough to motivate pupils to overcome them. This lesson comprises a number of exercises but no target movement. Each exercise can be regarded as a target movement and is a challenge in itself.

1. Warm-up

No.	Activity	P	Materials	Illustration
Running exercise				
1	1 Run one circuit while dribbling a tennis ball, using only one foot. Only use either the left or the right foot to control the ball. **Note:** *Keep the ball as close to your foot as possible to keep it under control and so as not to be a hindrance to others.*		1 tennis ball	
2	As with 1, but alternating between the left foot and the right foot.		1 tennis ball	
3	As with 1 but running backwards, keeping the tennis ball under the sole of one foot. **Note:** *Hop in short, sliding steps.*		1 tennis ball	
4	As with 1, but dribble the tennis ball and when told to do so by the instructor, stop and hop forwards/backwards over the tennis ball. Then continue running with the ball.		1 tennis ball	
5	As with 1, but dribble the tennis ball and when told to do so by the instructor, stop and run round it once – then continue running with the ball.		1 tennis ball	

Warm-up course: See end of lesson: Warm-up course - Assembly 13

2. 1. Climbing – Grimper

Materials: Large boxes, small boxes, crash mats, bench, ropes, wall bars/ladder.

Climb up the gap between the wall and the box. Hold onto the box and wall with one foot and one hand each, and progress up the wall by alternating sides.

Using the same movement, press your feet against the box and hold onto the wall by pressing your hands and back against it.

Exercises

Hang from the first-floor railing and clamber up the wall.

Use the grip holes in the boxes as steps.

Place and secure a bench longways against wall bars or ladder, with a crash mat in safety position. Hold on to the foot of the bench with the hands and walk along the underside of the bench top

Variation: Hold on to the foot of the bench with the hands and walk along the foot of the bench.

Materials: Table, horse, large box, benches, crash mat, landing mats.

1. Suspend two benches horizontally over a crash mat, hang beneath the benches and climb from the underside to the top.

2. Hold on to the top with one hand. Support yourself with one leg, bent at the knee.

3. Pull your body up to the front side by pushing off with the side leg.

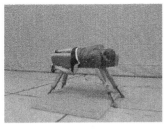

1. Climb through underneath a horse from one side to the other.

2. Move beneath the horse using hands and feet, without touching the floor.

3. Climb back onto the top of the horse.

1. Climb beneath a table from one side to the other.

2. Move beneath the table using hands and feet, without touching the floor.

3. Climb back onto the top of the table.

2. | **2. Muscle up – Planche**

Materials: Horizontal bar, bench, landing mats, crash mats, large boxes.

1. Push yourself up with the aid of an overhigh box alongside a horizontal bar that is overhead but within reach …

2. … by applying an explosive reduction of the arm-torso angle, supported by a push-off from the foot …

3. … and climb onto the box. Then jump onto the crash mats.

1. Push yourself up with the aid of a bench end-suspended on a horizontal bar at a height that is within reach …

2. … by applying an explosive reduction of the arm-torso angle …

3. … and run back down the secured bench.

Exercises

Exercises

2. **3. Seat drop and flip into sitting position**

Materials: Small boxes, large box, crash mats, landing mats, spectator stand/wall ladder.

Exercises

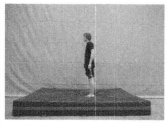  

1. Perform a seat drop from standing: stand in the middle of a crash mat with legs closed.

2. Take off strongly from the crash mat and bring the legs into a horizontal position. Bend the torso back slightly (keeping hip angle at around 110°) and move the arms back. Keep the palms of the hands pointing down.

3. Land on the crash mat along the entire length of the legs and at the same time on the palms, with the fingers pointing towards the feet, and the hands in a staggered position behind the buttocks.

1. Additionally secure the stack of crash mats by placing landing mats around the sides (ensure the jumping distance does not exceed 1.5 metres, to avoid the risk of compression injury). Push off from the railing or a ladder with a long-reaching step ...

2. ... Bring the legs into a horizontal position (maintain body tension!).

3. Keep the arms at the sides of the body and on landing place the hands behind and to the sides of the buttocks, with the fingertips pointing forward and the elbows slightly bent. The torso should be bent slightly backwards and the hip angle should be between 100° and 110°. The legs and feet should be closed and outstretched.

1. Perform a two-legged take-off from the railing.

2. Perform a front flip.

3. Land in a sitting position.

3. **Suggested games:** Not necessary due to the great demands of the main activity.

4. **Relaxation:** See ch. 9, exercises

Warm-up course   Assembly 13

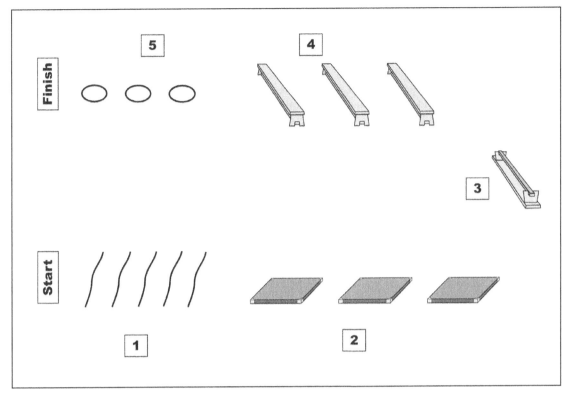

Number	Materials	Number	Materials
4	Benches	5	Skipping ropes
3	Hoops	3	Gymnastics mats

Stage	Object of exercise	Explanation
Start		Participants pass through the course individually, progressing from start to finish.
1	Jumping power	Jump forwards over two ropes with legs closed. Then jump backwards over one rope and forwards again over two ropes, etc.
2	Coordination and arm-support strength	Perform a forward roll on the first mat then dive over each space moving into a roll onto the next mat (dive roll).
3	Coordination	Balance along an upturned bench. Perform a total of three whole turns about the body's axis.
4	Coordination and jumping power	Jump over the first bench and land on one leg. Hop on this leg up to the next bench and jump over it. Land on the other leg and continue hopping on this leg. Hop over the third bench on one leg.
5	Coordination	Pick up each hoop individually and climb through it. Put each hoop back where it was.

Lesson 14   Wall Spin Backwards and Obstacle Roll

Introduction

The backward wall spin is another artistic move that originates from freerunning. It requires more co-ordination skill than the forward wall spin. There will be many pupils who are only able to complete the exercises up to the inclined crash mat stage. Only the most talented pupils will be able to perform the target movement. However, since at least the introductory exercises are relatively easy to perform (box exercises), the move can be regarded as relevant.

The obstacle roll is found both in parkour and freerunning since it is an effective means of overcoming obstacles (over a wide plateau) and is also frequently performed for enjoyment. The level of difficulty is not especially high but it requires a high level of coordination and a good ability to estimate distances. This lesson is also useful for practising and repeating all movements in preparation for the ensuing test lessons.

1. Warm-up

No.	Activity	P	Materials	Illustration
Running exercise				
1	Run back and forth between different lines on the floor of the hall: every fourth step, touch your buttocks with the right heel only. Then change legs. **Note:** *Run from one end of the hall to the other and back again.*	1	-	
2	As with 1, but alternating between the left and right heel **Note:** *Run from one end of the hall to the other and back again.*	1	-	
3	As with 1 and 2, but with high knees and swinging arms. **Note:** *Run from one end of the hall to the other and back again.*	1	-	

Warm-up course: See end of lesson: Warm-up course - Assembly 14

2. 1. Wall spin backwards

Materials: Wall, landing mats.

Target movement

1. Take a run-up at a 45° angle to the wall, keeping the eyes fixed on the outwardly turned hand, which touches the wall at chest height.

2. Pull up the inner leg with a powerful swing while at the same time throwing up the free arm. Take off using the foot furthest away from the wall. Keep watching the hand touching the wall. Rotate with legs bent at the knees, in a step position.

3. Land near the take-off point. The hand continues to hold onto the wall for support.

Materials: Large box (four-section), crash mat, landing mats.

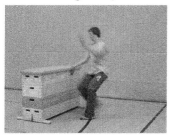  

1. Four-section box:
Stand to the side of a four-section box in step position. Keep the eyes focused on the outwardly turned hand (palm facing upwards). Take off from the leg furthest from the box.

2. Swing the leg nearest the box steeply upward, bent at the knee, landing with the foot on the box. The hand maintains contact with the box. The gaze is over the shoulder (here: right) towards the supporting hand.

3. Land on the front of the box (take-off side). In further repetitions, attempt to land further towards the middle of the box, until the supporting hand is now behind the body as it holds onto the box

 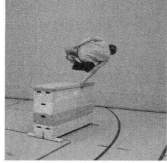 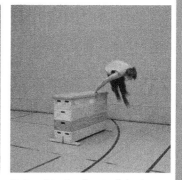

1. Box exercise: Take a short run-up to the box at a 45° angle with no interim jump. Pull up the inner leg with a powerful swing while at the same time throwing up the free arm. Keep the eyes focused on the supporting hand.

2. Both legs are tucked up and swung over the box, with the eyes still fixed on the supporting hand.

3. Land to the front of the box (take-off side). The hand keeps in contact with the edge of the box.

1. Tilted crash mat:
Take a run-up at a 45° angle. The hand nearest the wall is turned outward and the eyes are focused on the outreaching hand.

2. Push off from the floor with the with the foot furthest from the wall. Swing up the inner leg, keeping it bent at the knee, and keeping the eyes fixed on the supporting hand.

3. Land with closed legs with the hand still held against the crash mat for support.

Exercises

2. **2. Obstacle roll**

Materials: Landing mats, large box.

Target movement

1. Take a short run-up and perform a long take-off on one leg sideways towards the box. Move the shoulder nearest the box towards the box. At the moment of take-off, swing the free leg fast and strongly upward.

2. Set the shoulder area down on the top of the box. Allow the legs to swing over the box, bent slightly at the knee, about a hip distance apart
Note: Only place the shoulder girdle on the box when turning.

3. Swing the legs and turn into a standing position behind the box. Land behind the box sideways on with feet about hip-wide.

Materials: Landing mats, mat trolley.

Exercises

1. Perform a sideways roll on the floor: lower the torso towards the floor in a step position until you are touching the floor with the back of one arm (here: left).

2. Perform a sideways roll over your entire back, keeping the chin tucked into the chest.

3. Use the swing of the roll to come into a standing position.

1. Obstacle roll over a mat trolley: Perform a single-legged, long take-off sideways to the mat trolley.

2. Land on the mat trolley with the shoulder area only. Use the swing of the legs to roll over the mats.

3. Land behind the mats standing sideways on, with legs apart at hip distance.

3. **Suggested games:** Not necessary due to the great demands of the main activity.

4. **Relaxation:** See ch. 9, exercises

Warm-up course   Assembly 14

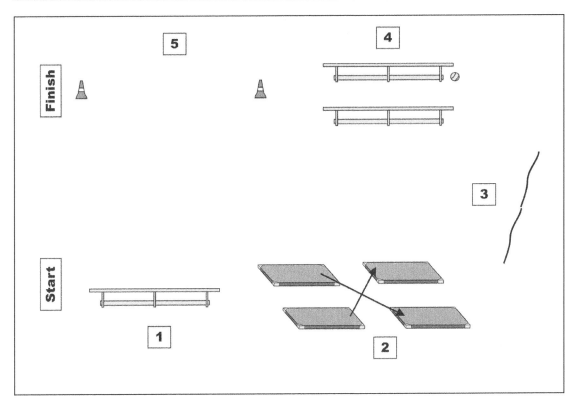

Number	Materials	Number	Materials
3	Benches	4	Gymnastics mats
2	Cones	2	Skipping ropes
3	Tennis balls		

Stage	Object of exercise	Explanation
Start		The course is run through from start to finish. Two participants start as a team.
1	Coordination	The two partners run one behind the other over the bench. The first runs backwards and the second runs forwards, with the hands in contact at chest height.
2	Coordination	Each performs a backward roll then crosses over to the next mat and performs a forward roll.
3	Coordination	Begin one after the other: hold the left foot onto the buttocks with the right hand and jump in a zigzag on one leg over the ropes, positioned one behind the other.
4	Coordination	Each partner runs sideways along a bench, throwing the tennis ball backwards and forwards one to the other (benches are approx. 3 m apart). Return the tennis ball to the start after completing.
5	Sprinting power	When given the joint instruction to start, race against your partner in a sprint.

Lesson 15   Timed Parkour Exercises

Introduction

There is a distinct sub-discipline of parkour, most commonly known as parcouring, in which the focus is on overcoming an obstacle course against the clock, generally within an organised competition. However, school lessons can also incorporate elements of parcouring, for example as a basis by which to award grades or scores. The assessment should not focus so much on the way an obstacle is tackled or on the quality of the moves a pupil selects, but simply on whether a pupil is able to overcome an obstacle or not. The teacher could consider involving pupils at an early stage in devising an appropriate apparatus course. This means that the assemblies described in the following should be regarded merely as suggestions. The teacher may also attach conditions to some apparatus stages, such as specifying that a certain apparatus is to be tackled by crawling, or requiring a vault to be followed by a roll, for example. It is essential that all the participants in a group are capable of overcoming all the obstacles. The aim, after all, is only to obtain comparative time scores.
There are several ways of achieving this:

1. Overcoming a specified course using non-standardised techniques.
2. Overcoming a specified course taking into account certain conditions (see 2.).
3. Overcoming a course devised by pupils using non-standardised techniques.
4. Overcoming a course devised by pupils taking into account certain conditions.

For scoring suggestions, see: www.parkoursport.com -> Materials

1. Warm-up

No.	Activity	P	Materials	Illustration
Running exercise				
1	Walk one circuit briskly with long steps, swinging the arms for support.	1	-	
2	The circuit contains four square zones (max. 4mx4m) marked out by cones. Whenever you are within any of these zones, switch from long steps to short, fast steps. **Note:** *Pupils should spread themselves out evenly throughout the area.*	1	Cones	
3	As with 2: Run round the circuit; when you are in one of the zones, perform a stretch jump.	1	Cones	
4	As with 2: Run round the circuit; when you are in one of the zones, spin about your body's axis, once to the right and once to the left.	1	Cones	

Warm-up course: See end of lesson: Warm-up course - Assembly 15

2. Timed parkour exercises (see next page)

3. Suggested games: Equipment rounders (see Game 4)

4. Relaxation: See ch. 9, exercises

2. Timed parkour exercises

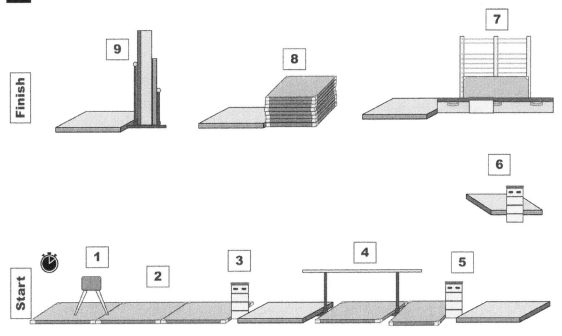

Number	Materials	Number	Materials	Number	Materials
1	Buck	1	Asymmetrical bars	1	Small box
3	Large boxes	13	Gymnastics/landing mats	1	Pile of mats
1	Parallel bars	1	Wall bars	1	Crash mat
1	Stopwatch				

Stage	Object of exercise	Explanation
Start		Participants pass through the course individually, progressing from start to finish. The external dimensions of the course are about the same as a volleyball field. The timing starts when the first mat is touched and ends when the landing mat behind the asymmetrical bars is touched.
1	Coordination	Crawl beneath the horse.
2	Roll	Roll over the mats.
3	Passement	Climb onto the box and jump off from there, or jump directly over it.
4	Balancing	Take up an arm-support position between the bars and dismount to the side over one bar. Then crawl back underneath and between the bars and climb onto the bars from the inside. Jump from the bars onto the box.
5	Drop	Jump from the box onto the landing mat.
6	Passement	Climb over the longways box.
7	Arm jump	Jump from a small box in front of the sideways positioned crash mat on to the wall bars. Then jump from the bars onto the side-positioned landing mat, without touching the crash mat.
8	Passement	Jump or climb over the mats.
9	Passement	Climb over the wall of crash mats (made up of mats placed between the parallel bars).

Warm-up course   **Assembly 15**

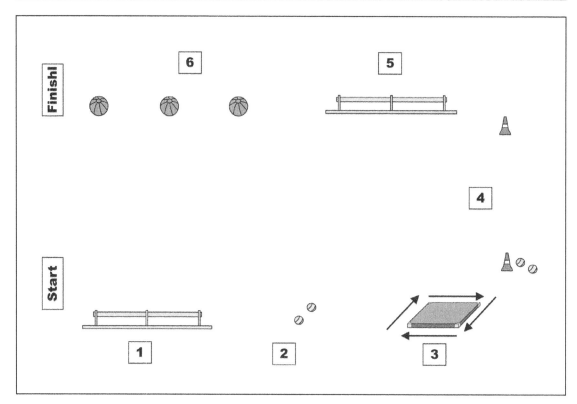

Number	Materials	Number	Materials
3	Medicine balls	8	Tennis balls
2	Benches	1	Gymnastics mat
2	Cones		

Stage	Object of exercise	Explanation
Start		Participants pass through the course individually, progressing from start to finish.
1	Coordination	Jump along the upturned bench on the right leg in small jumps.
2	Coordination	Throw the tennis ball straight up in the air, perform a whole turn around the body's axis and then catch the ball.
3	Speed and coordination	Stand on the front, right corner of the gymnastics mat and run quickly sideways to the left-hand corner. Then run forwards and again sideways along the long side. Then run backwards along the final short side to return to the start.
4	Coordination	Dribble a tennis ball between the cones while throwing another tennis ball straight up and catching it again.
5	Jumping power	Jump along the upturned bench on the left leg in small jumps.
6	Power endurance and coordination	Run from one medicine ball to the other, and squat down to touch each medicine ball in turn with your buttocks.

Lesson 16   *Parkour sports and Performance*

The discipline of freerunning combines elements of parkour with performance aspects. The main emphasis is on performing spectacular and complex movements. To be able to assess such moves, pupils need to be given a selection of apparatus stages that comprise several move options. They do not all necessarily have to be used and some can be used more than once. Pupils should be allowed to construct their own apparatus and to decide if any changes or additions need to be made. General rules can be laid down to aid the assessment of individual attempts, such as:

- The time must not exceed 45 seconds;
- A move may be performed once only;
- At least four different apparatus stages must be used;
- The various stages must be connected with running.

The assembly shown here is intended as a suggestion only. It is suitable for different abilities and for performing different moves. However, pupils are more likely to accept the exercises if they can be discussed once a number of practice runs have been completed (which the pupils would need to perform anyway). The extent to which changes to a run are permitted should also be determined in advance.

1. Warm-up

No.	Activity	P	Materials	Illustration
Running exercise				
1	Run one circuit with knees bent forwards (high knees).	1	-	
2	Run two circuits slowly, interspersed with short sprints (about 5m) when told to do so by the instructor.	1	-	
3	Two partners run sideways close to each other, passing a tennis ball from one to the other as often as possible. **Note:** *Begin by receiving the ball before returning it and move onto passing it back directly.*	2	Tennis balls	
4	As 3, but throwing the ball.	2	Tennis balls	

Warm-up course: See end of lesson: Warm-up course - Assembly 16

2. Parkour sports and performance (see next page)

3. Suggested games: Not necessary due to the great demands of the main activity.

4. Relaxation: See ch. 9, exercises

2. Parkour sports and performance

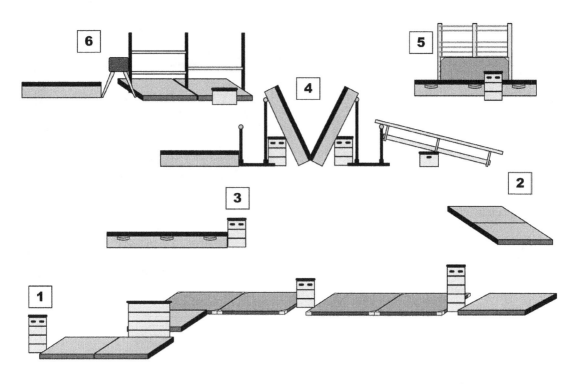

Number	Materials	Number	Materials	Number	Materials
1	Double bars	2	Small boxes	5	Gymnastics mats
1	Bar, hip height	8	Landing mats	1	Large box (5 section)
1	Wall bars	6	Crash mats	5	Large boxes (3 section)
2	Asymmetrical bars	1	Bench	2	Large boxes (4 section)
1	Buck	1	Skipping rope		

Stage	Explanation
Start	Participants pass through the course individually, progressing from start to finish. The external dimensions of the course are about the same as a volleyball field.
1	Boxes of different heights are set at varying distances to allow different jump combinations.
2	Landing mats are positioned close to a wall for wall runs, flips and spins.
3	A box is positioned alongside a crash mat for rolling over after completing an obstacle or for rollover movements.
4	Asymmetrical bars combination for overcoming obstacles. **Note:** *Fasten the bench to a bar with a rope and fix a small, sturdy box for support.*
5	Crash mat and boxes are set in front of wall bars for arm jumps.
6	Bar combination for dash vault, underbar, reverse vault, etc.

Warm-up course   Assembly 16

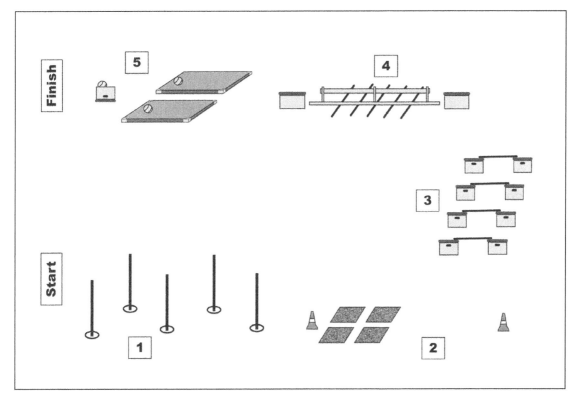

Number	Materials	Number	Materials
5	Poles and stands	11	Small boxes
4	Carpet tiles	5	Balance bars
2	Cones	1	Bench
2	Gymnastics mats	6	Tennis balls

Stage	Object of exercise	Explanation
Start		Participants pass through the course individually, progressing from start to finish.
1	Speed	Run slalom around the staggered poles.
2 (2)	Coordination	Stand with both feet on the front carpet tile supported by both hands on the rear carpet tile. Then slide forwards with the rear carpet tile and slide up with the feet on the other carpet tile.
3	Jumping power	Perform closed-leg jumps over balance bars laid on benches.
4*	Coordination	Balance on the rolling bench.
5 (2)	Coordination	Lie face down on a mat and throw the tennis ball into the box from this position (1 attempt only).

* = critical exercise (constant supervision required)
( ) = the number of apparatus assemblies recommended to avoid waiting times

Lesson 17   Theory unit: Parkour and Freerunning

Introduction

This theoretical unit has been conceived to be worked through at any stage of a course of instruction in practical parkour moves. It can form part of a general introduction to the topic or it can be covered once pupils have had a chance to gather some experience of the moves, for instance for studying movement analysis in more detail. The unit is divided into three sections: film analysis, movement analysis, and tips on obtaining information from the Internet. It would require about three double lessons to incorporate all three of these sub-modules in a course, however, each section can also be covered singly.

The theoretical material is all the more important in long-term courses with sixth-form classes, because it not only covers general sports theory, but also goes into the differences between the various disciplines, and points out how important the aspect of responsibility is when performing moves in public spaces.

As for the film analysis component, there are several films that have been made on the subject; however, the reasons why this documentary in particular has been chosen (Parkour: Way of Life; PARKOUR GENERATIONS) are that it presents an extensive treatment of both disciplines and is intended to be of particular interest to school pupils. Furthermore, the film points out to great effect how important it is to take part in constant training before attempting to perform more spectacular jumps. This is an important thing to realise, since pupils must never attempt to perform any exercises without adequate training and safety provisions, even if they expect them to be straightforward.

As an alternative to the film, pupils can conduct an Internet research activity (see the Internet addresses in chapter 9). It should be noted that the films listed in the reference section are not suitable for theoretical treatment, since they consist of little more than a few action-oriented parkour scenes, typical of those commonly presented by the film industry.

Additional theoretical work may take the form of movement analysis. This can involve actually filming moves during lessons, selecting film sequences from documentaries or obtaining them from the Internet. It is also useful to compare certain moves to point out any significant variations between and within them (see Worksheet 2). Interesting examples would be the roll or simple vaults, such as the lazy vault or speed vault.

The third option, the Internet research activity plus any open questions, can be conducted in the form of a project. The aim is to seek answers to questions that do not allow direct responses but require pupils to formulate their individual viewpoints, thus allowing them to better understand the various disciplines and the differences between them. The task should be reasonably easy to complete, as virtually all current discussions and media relating to parkour are disseminated through the Internet. By evaluating video films, forum threads, articles and interviews, these activities can produce a variety of different findings.

1. Worksheet 1: Film analysis: Parkour: Way of Life (Parkour Generations - 53 minutes, see Appendix)

2. Worksheet 2: Movement analysis and methodology in parkour (see Appendix)

3. Discussion exercises involving literature and Internet research (see Appendix)

Worksheet   Film analysis: Parkour - way of life

1.   From what city and country does parkour originate?

2.   What are the distinctive and characteristic features of parkour and freerunning?
     Parkour:

     Freerunning:

3.   What are the primary techniques and moves of each of these disciplines?
     Parkour:

     Freerunning:

4.   What other factors, in addition to the sports aspect, motivate practitioners into performing parkour?

5.   What principles must always be adhered to with regard to one's body?

6.   What principles must the practitioner adhere to when performing moves in public?

7.   To what extent are sports halls useful for freerunners?

8.   What are the central skills that must be acquired by a parkour practitioner and how does he train for them?

9.   To what does the parkour philosophy refer?

10.   What risks are associated with the performance of parkour?

Worksheet   Solutions: Film analysis: Parkour: way of life (53 Min.)

1. **From what city and country does parkour originate**
   - From Lisses, a suburb of Paris, France.
   - The founding group called themselves 'Yamakasi'

2. **What are the distinctive and characteristic features of parkour and freerunning?**
   Parkour:
   - Efficiency of movement
   - Requires intensive consideration of the sense of the moves
   Freerunning:
   - Acrobatic movements with turns
   - Spectacular, impressive moves, performed in public
   - Availability of more movements means there are more options for combining moves

3. **What are the primary techniques and moves of each of these disciplines?**
   Le Parkour: kong vault, precision vault, cat leap etc.
   Freerunning: flips (wall flip, aerial twist, front flip, side flip, gainer) etc.

4. **What other factors, in addition to the sports aspect, motivate practitioners into performing parkour?**
   - The sense of 'feeling alive'
   - A desire to escape
   - To prove that you can do it (developing self-confidence)
   - Discovering your limits

5. **What principles must always be adhered to?**
   - Never ignore sensations of fear
   - Commit to intensive training and practice simple moves often

6. **What principles must the practitioner adhere to when performing moves in public?**
   - Respect the obstacle
   - Respect other people and the environment
   - Performing moves without fear, and otherwise practising in systematic steps

7. **To what extent are sports halls useful for freerunners?**
   - Jumps are often perfected in the hall before they are performed outdoors

8. **What are the central skills that must be acquired by a parkour practitioner and how does he train for them?**
   - Long-term, intensive training, comprising in particular arm strength exercises (support and holding power) and agility
   - Mental and physical strength

9. **To what does the parkour philosophy refer?**
   - Parkour is a metaphor for life in general
   - Living in harmony with the environment
   - Using body and mind
   - Fluid motion and body control (absolute command)
   - Moving efficiently from one place to another
   - Perceiving the world as a playground
   - Developing an individual style and path
   - Enhancement of self-confidence and satisfaction

10. **What risks are associated with the performance of parkour?**
    - Overestimating one's ability, hence risking injury
    - Injury due to insufficient practice
    - Upsetting people who feel disturbed by the activities

| **Worksheet** | Movement analysis and methodology in parkour | |

1. Describe the phases of the roll as shown in the pictures. Use the following terms (given in no particular order): *Step position, head, knee-stand, shoulder and arm, diagonal, weight shifting*

2. a) What differences do you notice in the movement steps of the speed vault?
   b) In what ways can both movements be said to be effective (i.e. worthwhile in relation to the effort)?

3. Choose two exercises that can be useful in teaching beginners to perform a roll, and give reasons for your choices!

Worksheet | Solutions: Movement analysis and methodology in parkour

1. **Describe the phases of the roll as shown in the pictures. Use the following terms (given in no particular order):** *Step position, head, knee-stand, shoulder and arm, diagonal, shifting weight*

1. In the *step position, shift the weight* to the front leg and move the hands toward the ground. Place the front arm (here: left) on floor with the underside downward. Incline the *head* slightly to the side and tuck the chin into the chest.

2. Roll over *shoulder and arm* (here: left) *diagonally* over the back. After completing the rolling motion tuck one leg up (here: right) below the buttocks.

3. Straighten into a *knee-stand* on the bent leg.

4. Stretch the free leg out forwards and set down with the sole completely on the floor. Push up into a standing position from this step position and continue running.

2. **a) What differences do you notice in the movement steps of the speed vault?**
   b) In what ways can both movements be said to be effective (i.e. worthwhile in relation to the effort)?

2 a) First sequence of images: speed vault with one-armed support phase.
Second sequence of images: speed vault with double-armed support phase to reinforce the push-off.
2 b) The single-arm support phase is generally sufficient and efficient with short obstacles. However, for longer obstacles, it may be necessary to use the second arm for extra support or if the push-off from the floor or box was not strong enough to avoid touching the obstacle (aspect of effectiveness).

3. **Choose two exercises that can be useful in teaching beginners to perform a roll, and give reasons for your choices!**
   1. Begin performing the roll motion from a knee-stand position, to minimise the drop height and to be able to control the contact of the shoulder and arm with the ground without the risk of falling.
   2. Learn the roll movement, using a partner for help. The partner holds the pupil's hip in a clamp grip while the pupil lowers his hands towards the floor and slowly guides the motion, preventing the pupil's body from collapsing out of position.

3. **Discussion exercises involving literature and Internet research**

1. On what is the fascination that many sports people and the media have for parkour und freerunning based?

2. What are the various motives that practitioners may have to perform a parkour discipline?

3. What are the dangers associated with parkour und freerunning?

4. To what extent is it justified to refer to parkour as a trend sport?

5. Using examples, outline the different ways that the term 'parkour' is used.

6. Discuss whether it makes sense to transfer parkour and freerunning into the competition-based structure of a typical sports club.

7. Describe the acceptance of parcouring and freerunning among supporters of traditional parkour, using various statements expressed by parkour supporters.

8. Give a judgement as to whether attempting to perform a discipline in accordance with its philosophy in a sports hall can still be classified as real parkour or freerunning.

9. Using several examples, show that gymnastics can be seen to represent the origin of parkour and freerunning.

10. Give a reasoned prognosis of the position that parkour will assume in the future both in the sporting world and in society in general.

11. Using several examples, point out the ways in which parkour is being commercialised, and outline the advantages and disadvantages of this.

12. Explain the role that the Internet plays in parkour.

8. Parkour Games

No.	Name	No. of Players	Materials
1	Throw-off	Any	Benches, ceiling ropes, crash mats, soft balls, small boxes, asymmetrical bars, landing mats, large boxes

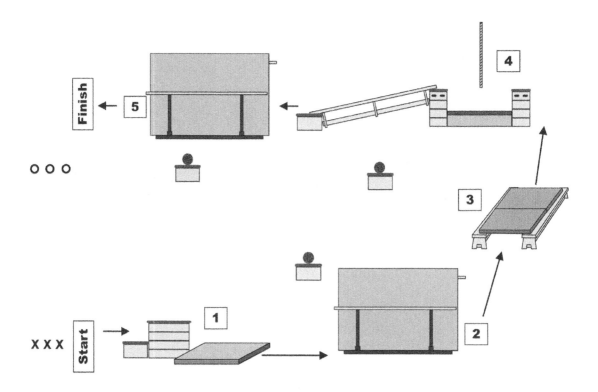

Stage	Explanation
1	Run over the boxes.
2	Run behind an upright crash mat clamped between asymmetrical bars.
3	Crawl beneath the landing mats that have been placed above two benches.
4	Swing from box to box with the ceiling rope and then balance along the bench.
5	Run behind an upright crash mat clamped between asymmetrical bars.

Two teams play against each other. The running team stands at the start line and the throwing team stands around the edge of the field. Once the game commences, the throwers play in the area inside the course. A maximum of three runners can be on the course at any one time. Once the signal is given to start, three throwers run into the field, each taking up a position on a box. Each thrower has one attempt to throw a soft ball at a runner and throw him off the course. Whether or not the ball hits the opponent, the thrower then returns to his team and the next player enters the field, retrieves the ball, stands on the box, and throws the ball. When a player from the running team is thrown off the course, he returns to his team and is replaced by the next player. When a runner reaches the finish without being thrown off the course, his team is awarded one point. After a set time (e.g. 5 minutes), the teams swap over. The team with the most points wins.

No.	Name	No. of Players	Materials
2	Equipment catch	Any	All equipment

In this game, players are free to use any available equipment they wish. The equipment is assembled throughout the hall to form a landscape. Mats are laid out on the floor spaces in-between to allow players to reach the equipment without touching the floor. One or two players are catchers, and their aim is to catch players on the equipment. The other players on the equipment have to resist the catchers' attempts to catch them. If a player is caught or if he touches the floor, he must perform 20 skips with a rope next to the playing field. The catchers aim to keep as many players as possible out of the apparatus course at any one time. The smallest number of players remaining in the course at the same time is noted. After two minutes, the catchers are replaced by two new ones.

No.	Name	No. of Players	Materials
3	Shoot-out	Any	Large boxes, crash mats, ceiling ropes, small boxes, gymnastics mats, benches, soft balls

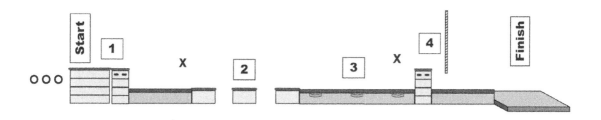

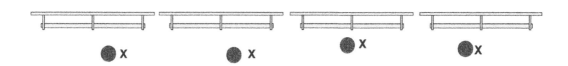

Stage	Explanation
1	Two large boxes are arranged at an angle: The first box is for protection while the second box is the one that has to be overcome by the starter. A crash mat is positioned behind it, in a sideways position.
2	Players have to run over the small boxes without touching the floor.
3	They then run over the crash mat.
4	Players climb on the large box and grip the ceiling rope. They then swing with the ceiling rope onto the gymnastics mat without touching the crash mat.

Two teams play against each other. The running team stands at the start, while the throwing team spreads out behind benches (7-9 m from the apparatus course). Each member of the throwing team has a soft ball, with which they must attempt to hit the runners. The runners attempt to clear the course in accordance with the rules (as given above) without being hit by a soft ball.

If a player is hit by a ball, he has to return to the start and begin again. Two neutral players from the throwing team are responsible for collecting the balls and throwing them back behind the benches. These players are, however, not allowed to throw players from the opposing team out. Each runner reaching the finish scores a point for his team. After a set time (e.g. 5 minutes) the teams change round. The team with the most points wins.

No.	Name	No. of Players	Materials
4	Equipment rounders	Any	Horizontal bar, crash mats, small boxes, landing mats, large box, soft ball, stopwatch

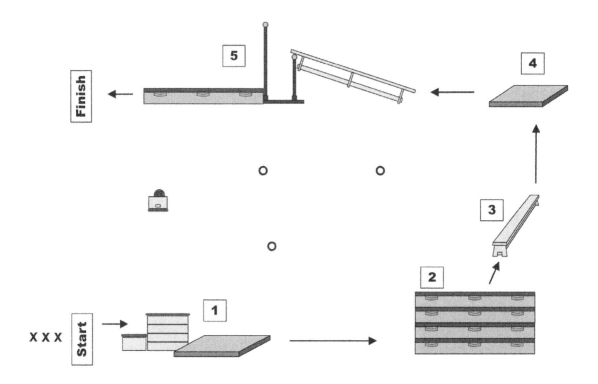

Stage	Explanation
1	Run over the staggered boxes and stand on the landing mat (rest point).
2	Climb onto the pile of crash mats (rest point).
3	Balance along the bench.
4	Stand on the landing mat (rest point).
5	Balance along the bench and perform a wall spin over the high horizontal bar, landing on the crash mat (rest point).

Two teams play against each other. The running team stands at the start and the throwing team stands in the space inside the course. The first runner throws a ball into the inside space and then attempts to progress as far as possible through the course before the throwing team either puts the ball in the small box or the runner is thrown off the course. Once a runner has reached a rest point he cannot be thrown out. If the throwing team manages to put the ball in the box before the runner has reached a rest point or the finish, the runner is out and returns to his team without scoring a point. Any number of running players may be in the course at any one time but only one person is allowed on each rest point.

Once a runner completes the course without being thrown out, his team gets one point. After a set time (e.g. 5 minutes) the teams change round. The team with the most points wins.

No.	Name	No. of Players	Materials
5	Timing	6 or more	Crash mats, gymnastics mats, large boxes, small boxes

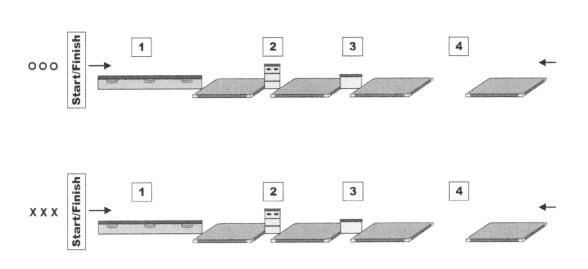

Stage	Explanation
1	Run longways over a crash mat.
2	Overcome a three-section box sideways.
3	Climb or jump longways over a small box.
4	Jump over the gap (about 2 m) between two mats.

At least three players from two or more teams stand at the starting line before an obstacle course, one behind the other. Before the game starts, the trainer states a time (e.g. 27 seconds). When the trainer gives the signal, the first player from each team begins the course, and attempts to complete it there and back within the given time. However, he must cross the finish line before the time runs out, or he will forfeit all the rounds that he has completed. Each outward and each return round scores one point. The rounds completed successfully within the time limit earn points for the entire team. The winner is the team whose runners complete the most rounds after all the players have had a turn.

No.	Name	No. of Players	Materials
6	Team run	6 or more	Large boxes, small boxes, landing mats, tennis balls, hoops, benches, ropes

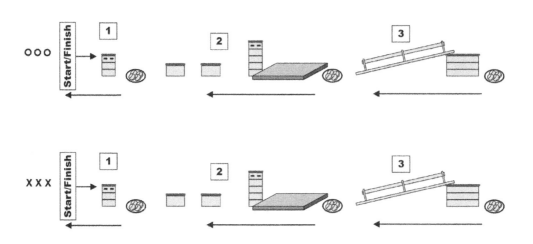

Stage	Explanation
1	Overcome a three-section box sideways.
2	Perform precision jumps from one box to the next (placed longways) and then overcome the high sideways-standing box.
3	Cat balance over a tilted upturned bench attached to a three-section longways-standing box.

Two or more obstacle courses of increasing difficulty are set up, each comprising three obstacle combinations. For each group, three hoops are laid in front of each obstacle, each containing a certain number of items (e.g. tennis balls). Either the group together or each player individually decides which hoop the player has to run to. The aim is to bring the balls back to the group as quickly as possible. Each player is only permitted to take one ball per run. The game involves a degree of self-assessment because it is up to each runner to work out which hoops can be reached by which players, bearing in mind their individual performance skills, to obtain the best group result.

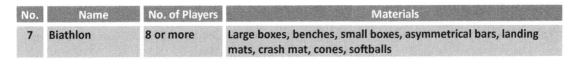

No.	Name	No. of Players	Materials
7	Biathlon	8 or more	Large boxes, benches, small boxes, asymmetrical bars, landing mats, crash mat, cones, softballs

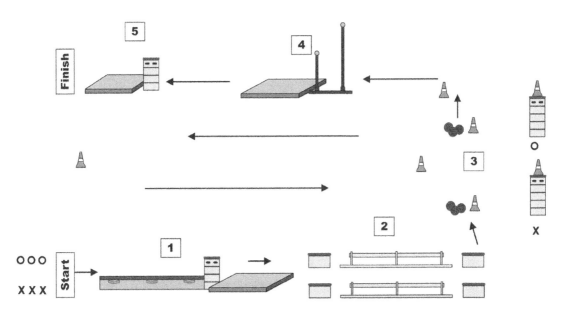

Stage	Explanation
1	Run over the crash mat and climb or jump over the sideways-standing box.
2	Walk and balance from a small box to an upturned bench and climb back onto the small box.
3	Throw three softballs onto three cones placed on a large sideways-standing box. For each miss, the player has to run a circuit from cone to cone (maximum of three penalty circuits). One player from each team stands next to the box and stands the cones back up for the next player.
4	Swing underbar through the asymmetrical bars from behind.
5	Overcome the large sideways box with a freely selected vault.

Two teams with the same number of players stand at the starting line. The first player from each team starts and runs through the course. Once a player has completed the course, the next player begins. The first team whose players all complete the biathlon course is the winner.

No.	Name	No. of Players	Materials
8	Running by numbers	6 or more	Poles and stands, crash mats, benches, small boxes, large boxes, dice

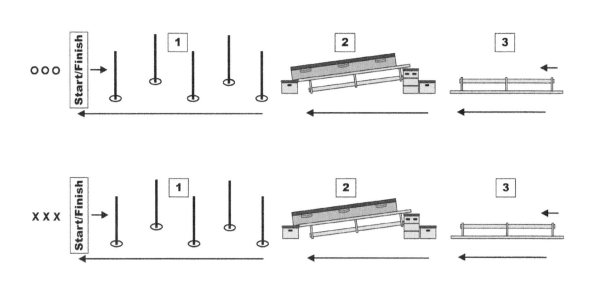

Stage	Explanation
1	Run through the pole slalom with your hands behind your back.
2	A crash mat lies over three benches resting on a three-section box. In front of and behind the box is at least one small sideways-standing box (the front box should preferably be three-section and sideways-standing). Run over the tilted crash mat and climb back down the descending boxes.
3	Balance along the upturned bench.

At least three players from two or more teams stand at the starting line before an obstacle course, one behind the other. The first player from each team throws the dice and performs the corresponding activity (see below) in the obstacle course, both outward and back. Once the player returns to his team, he touches the next player who then throws the dice to select an activity. The team whose runners all successfully complete one activity wins.
Alternatively:
Perform more than one successive run.
The team completing the highest number of rounds in a set time wins.

Dice scores and corresponding activities
1: First stage only, returning outside the obstacle.
2: Up to second stage, returning outside the obstacles.
3: Up to third stage, returning outside the obstacles.
4: First stage only, also returning through the obstacle.
5: Up to second stage, also returning through the obstacles.
6: Up to third stage, also returning through the obstacles.

9. Relaxation exercises

1. Torso – front

No.	Muscles	Exercise	Comments	Illustration
1	Chest muscles: *M. pectoralis major*	Hold on to a door frame or similar object with an outstretched arm or fix arm in position behind the back with the help of a partner. Take a step forward thus moving the torso forward, until a light tension is felt in the chest muscle area.	Carefully increase the tension by turning the free shoulder slightly outwards.	
2	External oblique stomach muscles: *M. obliquus externus abdominis* Chest muscles: *M. pectoralis major* Back muscles: *M. erector trunci*	Lie on your side: Bend knees and hips to over 90°. Hold the thigh of the uppermost leg onto the floor with the lower hand, maintaining a knee angle of about 90°. Twist the shoulder girdle away from the hip, keeping both shoulder blades touching the floor. External rotation of the upper arm increases the stretching effect of the chest muscles.	The exercise should be performed on a mat.	
3	Chest muscles: *M. pectoralis major* Upper arm muscles: *M. biceps brachii,* *M. triceps brachii*	Stand upright with legs apart at shoulder distance and bend the knees slightly. Place both hands on the back and pull downward and backward.	Keep the torso upright.	
4	Chest muscles: *M. pectoralis major* External oblique stomach muscles: *M. obliquus externus abdominis* Shoulder muscles: *M. deltoideus*	Stand on hands and knees with hips and arms forming angles of 90° with the torso. Stretch one arm out backwards and upwards. Keep looking at the outstretched arm.	The exercise should be performed on a mat.	
5	Chest muscles: *M. pectoralis major*	Kneel down on the floor and sit down between the feet. Then slowly stretch out the torso with the back to the floor, and arms outstretched. Maintain the position.	The exercise should be performed on a mat.	

2. Torso – back

No.	Muscles	Exercise	Comments	Illustration
6	*Back muscles:* *M. erector spinae lumbalis,* *M. erector spinae thoracalis*	Reach both arms beneath the knees from the inside and grip the insteps of the feet with the hands. Lower the head between the knees and rounden the back. Stretch out slowly at the knees.	Do not lose the contact between the hands and the feet while stretching.	
7	Lower back muscles: *M. erector spinae lumbalis*	Lie on your back. Bend one leg and pull knee up towards the chest with both hands placed below the knee joint. Keep the head and the other leg on the mat. Fix the eyes on the ceiling. Pull the foot up to the shin.	The exercise should be performed on a mat.	
8	Back muscles: *M. latissimus dorsi*	Lie on your back: Bend both legs and pull knees up towards the chest with both hands placed below the knee, while raising the head.	The exercise should be performed on a mat.	
9	Back muscles: *M. latissimus dorsi* Back leg muscles: *M. biceps femoris,* *M. semitendinosus,* *M. gastrocnemius*	Adopt a sitting position with legs outstretched: Try to touch the tips of your toes with your hands.	Keep the torso upright and keep the eyes fixed on the toes. Keep the knees straight.	
10	Straight back muscles: *M. latissimus dorsi,* *M. erector spinae lumbalis* Chest muscles: *M. pectoralis major*	Stand on your hands and knees. Slide arms far forward and push both shoulder joints towards the floor. Allow buttocks to rest on the heels.	The exercise should be performed on a mat.	
11	Upper back muscles: *M. trapezius*	Stand with the legs open at shoulder distance, and bend the knees slightly. Keep the head straight and look down towards the floor. Stretch both arms forwards at shoulder height. Push the back out.	Bend the elbows slightly outward.	

No.	Muscles	Exercise	Comments	Illustration
12	Upper back muscles: *M. trapezius*	Stand with the legs open at shoulder distance, and bend the knees slightly. Keep the head straight and look down towards the floor. Reach both hands round your chest to touch the opposite shoulders. Pull shoulders slightly forward and push them towards each other.	Keep the pelvis to the front.	
13	Back muscles: *M. erector spinae thoracalis,* *M. erector spinae lumbalis*	Kneel down and rest hands on floor with arms slightly bent. Keep legs a shoulder distance apart and arms likewise. Push the spine upward until the back is arched.	The exercise should be performed on a mat.	

3. Torso – hips and buttocks

No.	Muscles	Activity	Comments	Illustration
14	Posterior muscles: *M. glutaeus maximus*	Stretch out one leg and cross the other leg over it. Press the bent knee with the opposite elbow onto the outstretched leg, until you notice a light tension in the right posterior muscles. Turn the head towards the back and lean onto the free arm, with the free hand resting on the floor behind the body.	Keep the upper torso upright.	
15	Inner hip muscles: *M. adductor magnus,* *M. adductor longus,* *M. adductor minimus*	Sit down on a mat with legs crossed over and bent at the knees. Cross the arms and place your hands on your knees, pushing the knees lightly towards the floor.	The exercise should be performed on a mat. Keep the upper torso upright.	
16	Posterior muscles: *M. glutaeus maximus*	Lie on your back, with your body stretched out. Raise one leg to form a 90° angle and bend the knee. Push the foot of the other leg onto the thigh of the bent leg, just above the knee. Using both hands, hold the bent leg below the knee and pull lightly towards the chest.	The exercise should be performed on a mat.	

No.	Muscles	Exercise	Comments	Illustration
17	Front hip muscles: *M. iliopsoas*	Stand in a lunge position. Shift the weight onto the front leg, and bend this leg, ensuring that the knee of the standing leg stays above the foot. Press the pelvis down towards the front leg.	Keep the upper torso upright.	
18	Front hip muscles: *M. iliopsoas*	Kneel down on one leg and keep the other foot flatly on the floor, ensuring the angle between the two legs is not less than 90°. Push the hip carefully forwards and downwards.	Keep the upper torso upright. The exercise should be performed on a mat.	
19	Inner hip muscles (adductors): *M. gracilis, M. adductor longus, M. adductor brevis, M. pectineus*	Stand with one leg stretched out to the side and with the feet pointing forwards. Bend the other leg and move the pelvis diagonally downwards towards this leg.	Keep the upper torso upright and try not to place hands on the bent leg for support.	
20	Inner hip muscles: *M. adductor magnus, M. adductor longus, M. adductor minimus*	Sit with the soles of the feet together and pull them towards the buttocks. Press the legs down with the elbows, with the hands gripping the tips of the feet.	Keep the upper torso upright. Do not rock the legs but ease in the tension slowly.	
21	Back hip muscles: *M. glutaeus maximus, M. glutaeus medius, M. glutaeus minimus, M. tensor fasciae latae, M. piriformis, M. obturatorius internus, M. quadratus femoris, Mm. gemelli*	Stretch out one leg and cross the other leg over it. Pull the bent knee towards the chest.	Keep the upper torso upright. Keep the heel of the crossed leg on the floor.	

4. Torso – side

No.	Muscles	Exercise	Comments	Illustration
22	Lateral torso muscles: *M. obliquus externus abdominus*, *M. obliquus internus abdominus*, *M. quadratus lumborum*, *M. tensor fascie latae*	Stand upright with legs crossed over and arms hanging at your sides. Raise the arm on the side of the crossed-over leg, while bending upper torso slightly to the side. Slide the hip to one side and the torso to the other.	Allow the raised arm to touch the ear. The head should continue the body's smooth sideways stretch, with no bend in the neck.	
23	External oblique stomach muscles: *M. obliquus externus abdominis*	Stand with the legs open at shoulder distance. Bend the knees slightly and keep the hips pointing to the front. Raise the arms to shoulder height with the fingertips pointing towards each other and the elbows pointing outwards. Turn the torso with one elbow to one side, with the head following the motion.	Keep the pelvis to the front.	
24	External oblique stomach muscles: *M. obliquus externus abdominis*	Stand on your knees on a mat. Stand in a lunge position, with a knee angle of a little over 90°. Twist the torso towards the front foot and place the hand from the other side of the body on the outside of the knee. The other arm rests on the back, bent at the elbow.	The exercise should be performed on a mat. Keep the upper torso upright.	
25	Lateral torso muscles: *M. obliquus externus abdominus*, *M. obliquus internus abdominus*	Stand with the legs opened to shoulder distance. Stretch one arm down and slide hand downwards along the thigh. At the same time, stretch out the other arm upwards and over the head and bend the body to the side.	Avoid the pelvis making a yielding movement against the lateral inclination.	

5. Legs

No.	Muscles	Exercise	Comments	Illustration
26	Back leg muscles: *M. biceps femoris*, *M. semitendinosus*, *M. semimembranosus*, *M. gastrocnemius*, *M. soleus*	Bend the standing leg slightly and stretch the other leg with the heel touching the floor. Pull up the front of the foot and slide the pelvis slowly backwards, until the tension can be felt in the back of the thigh. Keep the back straight.	Keep the torso straight.	
27	Back thigh muscles: *M. biceps femoris*, *M. semitendinosus*, *M. semimembranosus*	Bend the legs slightly and stand with feet apart at shoulder distance. Bend forwards slowly and stretch the arms forwards and upwards to form a continuous line with the back.	Avoid arching the back.	
28	Back thigh muscles: *M. biceps femoris*, *M. semitendinosus*, *M. semimembranosus*	Stand on your knees and stretch one leg forward, bringing the foot to rest on the heel. Keep the torso straight and lean forward slightly. The shin of the rear leg rests evenly on the floor. Shift the weight of the upper torso slightly towards the rear heel, by carefully moving the buttocks backwards.	Avoid arching the back.	
29	Back lower leg muscles: *M. gastrocnemius*, *M. soleus*	Stand in a lunge position. Stretch out the rear leg with both feet pointing forwards. The back leg and the torso are in line with each other. Slide the pelvis towards the front knee and bend the torso forward slightly until a light tension can be felt in the calf.	Ensure the feet are in the correct position. Press the rear heel onto the floor.	

No.	Muscles	Exercise	Comments	Illustration
30	Back thigh muscles: *M. biceps femoris,* *M. semitendinosus,* *M. semimembra-nosus*	Stand with the legs parallel. Move one leg forward with no pressure on the heel. Bend the other leg at the knee and shift the weight of the torso slowly forwards.	Keep the torso straight.	
31	Front thigh muscles: *M. quadriceps femoris* *(M. rectus femoris,* *M. vastus medialis,* *M. vastus intermedius,* *M. vastus lateralis)*	Stand with the legs parallel. Pull the heel of one foot towards the buttocks with the same-side hand. Keep the knees at the same height alongside each other and the hip stretched. Bend the standing leg slightly at the knee.	Keep the upper torso upright.	
32	Front thigh muscles: *M. quadriceps femoris* *(M. rectus femoris,* *M. vastus medialis,* *M. vastus intermedius,* *M. vastus lateralis)*	Lie on your side on the floor. Bend the lower leg in front of the body and rest the head on the outstretched arm. Swing up the heel of the upper leg and hold onto the ankle with the hand of the upper arm, then pull towards the buttocks.	The exercise should be performed on a mat. Keep the bent leg in line with the torso.	
33	Back thigh muscles: *M. biceps femoris,* *M. semitendinosus,* *M. semimembra-nosus*	Stretch out the entire body and rest the head. Raise one outstretched leg towards the ceiling, holding onto the back of the thigh with both hands for support.	The exercise should be performed on a mat. The sole of the foot should point towards the ceiling and the heel of the other foot should keep touching the floor. Keep the knees straight.	

6. Arms

No.	Muscles	Exercise	Comments	Illustration
34	Back upper arm muscles: *M. triceps brachii*	Place one hand over the shoulder and press the elbow downwards with the other hand. *Alternatively:* Use the second hand to hold the first from below, and pull it downwards.	Do not press the head down into the chest but keep it straight.	

No.	Muscles	Exercise	Comments	Illustration
35	Lower arm muscles: *M. pronator teres,* *M. flexor carpi radialis,* *M. palmaris longus*	Place the hands on the floor, a shoulder length apart, with the fingers pointing towards the knees. Press the balls of the thumbs firmly onto the floor and bend the body as far as possible towards the heels until a tension spreads from the lower arms to the shoulders.	Allow the tension to grow gradually. Use a mat.	
36	Upper arm muscles: *M. triceps brachii,* *M. biceps brachii*	Stand with the legs a shoulder distance apart and bend slightly at the knees. Raise the hands above your head and interlock the fingers of both hands, pulling upward with the palms pointing towards the ceiling.	Keep the torso straight.	
37	Upper arm muscles: *M. triceps brachii,* *M. biceps brachii*	Sit with legs apart and stretched out. Keeping the torso upright and the hands interlocked, move the hands forward as far as possible, with the palms facing outwards.	Keep the upper torso upright.	

7. Shoulders and neck

No.	Muscles	Exercise	Comments	Illustration
38	Shoulder muscles: *M. deltoideus* Neck muscles: *M. trapezius,* *M. rhomboideus minor,* *M. rhomboideus major,* *M. levator scapulae*	Bend the head to one side and pull the arm of that side downward using the other arm.	Avoid bending at the hip.	

No.	Muscles	Exercise	Comments	Illustration
39	Shoulder muscles: *M. deltoideus*	Sit on the mat with legs crossed. Cross the arms over and touch the opposite shoulder blades with the hands. Pull gently on the shoulder blades.	The exercise should be performed on a mat. Keep the torso straight.	
40	Shoulder muscles: *M. deltoideus*	Stand with the legs a shoulder distance apart and bend slightly at the knees. Keep the head straight and the shoulders down. Touch the arm above the elbow with the hand of the other arm and push the length of the upper arm towards the chest.	Keep the elbow slightly bent. Avoid turning at the hip.	
41	Shoulder muscles: *M. deltoideus* *M. latissimus dorsi* *M. teres major*	Stand with legs together and stretch the arms out behind the back. Bend forward slowly until the torso is horizontal, and point the arms towards the ceiling (retroversion) until a tension can be felt in the shoulder joints.	Keep the torso straight.	

10. Bibliography and References

1. Internet addresses

ASSOCIATIONS

PARKOUR WORLDWIDE ASSOCIATION (PAWA)	**2009**	www.myparkour.com.
AUSTRALIEN PARKOUR ASSOCIATION	**2009**	www.parkour.asn.au.
KULTOS AG	**2009**	www.parcouring.com.

INFORMATION

EDWARDES, D.	**2009**	www.parkourgenerations.com.
MEYER, D. & A. KALTEIS	**2009**	Parkour Grundbewegungen, in: www.parkour.de/moves/.
PIOSIK, D.	**2009**	www.parkour-germany.de or www.parkour.de.
MÜLLER, A.	**2009**	www.freerunning.net.
TOOROCK, M.	**2010**	www.americanparkour.com.
WORLDWIDE JAM	**2010**	www.worldwidejam.tv/pkbasics.1.jam.parkour.html.

PORTRAITS

FOUCAN, S.	**2009**	www.foucan.com.
HESS, S.	**2009**	www.sandra-hess.com.

OTHER

Keyword „PARKOUR"	**2009**	www.youtube.de.
ACCIDENT INSURANCE ORGANISATION "UNFALLKASSE NRW"	**2009**	www.unfallkasse-nrw.de, search term: Parkour.

2. Films

DOCUMENTARIES

AMERICAN PARKOUR	**2009**	American Parkour Presents: Parkour Tutorial Volume 1.
ANGEL, J.	**2009**	Once is never: Training with Parkour Generations.
CHRISTIE, M.	**2004**	Jump London.
CHRISTIE, M.	**2005**	Jump Britain.
PARKOUR GENERATIONS	**2008**	Parkour: way of life.

CINEMA FILMS CONTAINING TYPICAL PARKOUR SEQUENCES

ALESSANDRIN, P.	**2009**	Ghettogangz 2: Ultimatum.
BESSON, L.	**2001**	Yamakasi.
KASSOVITZ, M.	**2008**	Babylon A. D.
MANN, S.	**2009**	The Tournament.
MOREL, P.	**2004**	Banlieu 13.

3. Bibliography

BAUMANN, N. & H. HUNDELOH	**1996**	Alternative Nutzung von Sportgeräten, Bundesverband der Unfallkassen, GUV, München.
BECKER, W., BOCKHORST, R. & K. HABERSTROH	**1998**	Hilfen zum Helfen – Helfergriffe für das Turnen in der Schule, Gemeindeunfallversicherungsverband Westfalen-Lippe, Münster.
BERTRAM, A.	**1967**	Deutsche Turnsprache – Einheitliche Übungsbezeichnungen im Gerätturnen, Limpert, Frankfurt a. Main.
BRUCKMANN, M.	**2000**	Wir turnen miteinander, Knirsch Verlag, Kirchentellinsfurt.
BUCHER, W.	**1982**	1008 Spiel- und Übungsformen im Gerätturnen, Verlag Karl Hofmann, Schorndorf.
EDWARDES, D.	**2009**	Parkour, Crabtree Publishing Company, New York.
EDWARDES, D.	**2009**	The Parkour & Freerunning Handbook, Virgin Books, London.
GERLING, I. E.	**2002**	Gerätturnen für Fortgeschrittene – vol. 1 Boden und Schwebebalken, Meyer & Meyer Verlag, Aachen.
GERLING, I. E.	**2008**	Gerätturnen für Fortgeschrittene – vol. 2 Sprung-, Hang- und Stützgeräte, Meyer & Meyer Verlag, Aachen.
GERLING, I. E.	**2006**	Kinder turnen – Helfen und sichern, Meyer & Meyer Verlag, Aachen.
GÖRING, A. & M. LUTZ	**2008**	Le Parkour – Zwischen Trend und Tradition, in: LandesSportBund Niedersachsen No. 4, pp. 16-17 & No. 5, pp. 22-23.
HAFENMAIR, T.	**1999**	Die Judorolle – Übungsbeispiele zum sicheren Fallen, in: Lehrerbriefe zur Unfallverhütung und Sicherheitserziehung, GUV, No. 4, ROT-GELB-GRÜN Verlag, Braunschweig.
HEINLIN, C.	**2008**	Parkour – L'art du déplacement, in: Sport Praxis vol. 49, issue 11, Limpert, Wiebelsheim.
IDE, J.	**2007**	Von der Hasenheide zum Freerunning, in: NTB-Magazin 06, p. 18.
KNIRSCH, K.	**2000**	Lehrbuch des Gerät- und Kunstturnens, vol. 1. Technik und Methodik in Theorie und Praxis für Schule und Verein, Knirsch-Verlag, Kirchentellinsfurt.
KNIRSCH, K.	**2001**	Gerätturnen mit Kindern, Knirsch-Verlag, Kirchentellinsfurt.
KNIRSCH, K. & S. LAUMANNS	**2007**	Turnen in der Schule und im Verein, Knirsch-Verlag, Kirchentellinsfurt.
KRICK, F.	**2008**	Le Parkour oder die Kunst der Fortbewegung, in: Sportpädagogik, issue 4/5, Friedrich-Verlag, Seelze, pp. 44-53.
LANGE, S. & K. BISCHOFF	**2006**	Doppelstunde Turnen – Unterrichtseinheiten und Stundenbeispiele für Schule und Verein, Hofmann-Verlag, Schorndorf.
LASSLEBEN, A.	**2007**	Tic Tac und Wallspin - Anregungen für den Trendsport Parkour, in: Sportpädagogik, issue 5, pp. 41-43.
LEYE, M.	**1993**	Sicherheit im Schulsport – Stützen, in: Lehrerbriefe zur Unfallverhütung und Sicherheitserziehung, No. 3, GUVV, ROT-GELB-GRÜN Verlag, Braunschweig.
LIEDTKE, S.	**2009**	„Le Parkour" & Freerunning – Hindernisse kreativ überwinden im Schulsport, in: Betrifft Sport, No. 3, Meyer & Meyer Verlag, Aachen, pp. 10-13.
LIEDTKE, S.	**2009**	Le Parkour – Von „basic moves" zum ersten „run"!, in: Betrifft Sport, No. 4, Meyer & Meyer Verlag, Aachen, pp. 19-31.

LINDEMANN, U.   **2009**   Le Parkour im Schulsport – Und was ist mit der Sicherheit, in: Betrifft Sport, No. 4, Meyer & Meyer Verlag, Aachen, pp. 7-11.

LUKSCH, M.   **2009**   Tracers Blackbook – Geheimnisse der Parkour Technik, ParkourONE, Bern.

LÜTGEHARM, R.   **2001**   Stundenbilder Sport – Spiel, Spaß und Spannung beim Geräteturnen, Kohl-Verlag, Kerpen.

MARTIN, K.   **2004**   Springen in seiner Vielfalt erleben (part 2), in: Leichtathletiktraining, vol. 15, issue 4, Münster, pp. 28-35.

MATROS, P.   **2010**   Trendsport „Parkour", in: Lehrhilfen für den sportunterricht, vol. 59, issue 4, Hofmann Schorndorf, pp. 1-7.

PAPE-KRAMER, S.   **2007**   Le Parkour, in: sportunterricht, vol. 56, issue 6, Hofmann Schorndorf, pp. 169-175.

SCHARENBERG, S.   **2007**   Spektakulär wie „Le Parkour" – Wandsalto und Salto rückwärts, in: Sport & Spiel, No. 28, Kallmeyer-Verlag, Seelze, pp. 28-33.

SCHARENBERG, S.   **2008**   Gerätturnen mit neuem Verbandsimage?, in: sportunterricht, vol. 57, issue 3, Hofmann Schorndorf, pp. 75-80.

SCHMIDT-SINNS, J.   **2008**   Lehrhilfen - Parkour - hier ist der Weg das Ziel, in: sportunterricht, vol. 57, issue 9, Hofmann Schorndorf, pp. 1-4.

SCHMIDT-SINNS, J.   **2009**   Parkour – Praktische Beispiele für eine einführende und schulgemäße Vermittlung (1), in: sportunterricht, vol. 58, issue 10, Hofmann Schorndorf, pp. 7-14.

SCHMIDT-SINNS, J. & S. SCHOLL   **2010**   Freerunning – mit Spin und Flip den Unterricht bereichern, in: Lehrhilfen für den sportunterricht, vol. 59, issue 2, Hofmann Schorndorf, pp. 5-13.

SCHULZ, A.   **2009**   Unterrichtsvorhaben – Le Parkour, erste Erfahrungen mit dem Überwinden von Hindernissen in einer fünften Klasse, in: Betrifft Sport, No. 4, Meyer & Meyer Verlag, Aachen, pp. 12-18.

SPORT THIEME   **2008**   Parkour – es gibt keine Hindernisse mehr, in: Volltreffer, issue 49, Thieme, Grasleben, pp. 4-5.

11.

A

Arm jump	79

B

Balance	44
Balancing	44
Basic roll	69

C

Cat leap	79
Cat balance	46
Centric	18
Clearing	62
Climbing	101
Crane jump	49

D

Dash vault	60
Demi tour	98
Dismount	47
Dive	73
Drop jump	69

E

Équilibre	44
Eccentric	18

F

Franchissement	62
Foot fight	44

G

Gap jump	85
Grimper	101

J

Jumping	101
Jump of the cat	51

K

King Kong vault	51
Kong vault	51

L

Lateral vault	52
Lazy vault	51
Lazy vault reverse	55

M

Mixed grip	98
Mixed grip, crossed	66
Monkey vault	51
Muscle up	103

O

Obstacle Roll	108
Overhand grip	62

P

Passement	51
Passe de barrière	51
Passe muraille	97
Planche	103
Power exercise	50
Precision jump	46

Q

Quadrupedal movement	17

R

Reverse vault	56
Roll	69
Roulade	69

S

Saut de bras	79
Saut de chat	51
Saut de fond	69
Saut de précision	46
Seat Drop	104
Speed vault	52
Split foot	19
Step vault	52
Swing up	93

T

Tic-tac	76
Turn vault	98

U

Underbar	62
Underbar, spiral	65

W

Wall flip	92
Wall run	76
Wall spin	87
Wall spin backwards	106
Wall up	80

Lightning Source UK Ltd.
Milton Keynes UK
UKOW05f1839271115

263671UK00005B/136/P